FENG SHUI

Principles for Building and Remodeling

*Creating a Space That Meets Your Needs
and Promotes Well-Being*

NANCILEE WYDRA, FSII,
author of *Feng Shui: The Book of Cures,*
and Lenore Weiss Baigelman, AIA, FSII

Contemporary Books

Chicago New York San Francisco Lisbon London Madrid Mexico City
Milan New Delhi San Juan Seoul Singapore Sydney Toronto

Library of Congress Cataloging-in-Publication Data

Wydra, Nancilee.
    Feng Shui principles for building and remodeling : creating a space that meets
your needs and promotes well-being / Nancilee Wydra, Lenore Weiss Baigelman.
        p.   cm.
    Includes index.
    ISBN 0-8092-9738-8 (alk. paper)
     1. Feng shui—Health aspects.   2. Mind and body.   3. Conduct of life.
  4. Self-care, Health.   I. Baigelman, Lenore Weiss.   II. Title.

RZ999 .W935   2002
  613—dc21

        2002067592

ADY-2763

1 2 3 4 5 6 7 8 9 0   QPD/QPD 1 0 9 8 7 6 5 4 3 2

ISBN 0-8092-9738-8

Cover and interior design by Nick Panos
Cover illustration by Nicholas Wilton/Images.com
Cover author photo by Samantha Baigelman
Text copyright © by Nancilee Wydra
Interior illustrations copyright © by Lenore Weiss Baigelman

McGraw-Hill books are available at special quantity discounts to use as premiums and
sales promotions, or for use in corporate training programs. For more information, please
write to the Director of Special Sales, Professional Publishing, McGraw-Hill, Two Penn
Plaza, New York, NY 10121-2298. Or contact your local bookstore.

Every effort has been made to ensure that the information contained in this book is as
complete and accurate as possible. However, the authors and publisher are not
responsible for any errors or omissions and no warranty or fitness is implied. This book is
sold with the understanding that the authors and publisher are not engaged in rendering
professional advice or services to the reader. Neither authors nor publisher shall bear
liability or responsibility to any person or entity with respect to any loss or damage arising
from information contained in this book.

This book is printed on acid-free paper.

To all who build dreams in the mold of structures, especially female architects like Lenore Weiss Baigelman and Tracy Taylor Wydra, who will bring the hearts of women into mortar and bricks, shaping not only individual lives but also civilizations.

—NANCILEE WYDRA

This book is dedicated to all of the exceptional teachers in my life who have helped shape the structure of my perspective: my foundation—Jerry, Naomi, and Marty Weiss; my framework—Danny and Nancilee; and my windows to the world, through whose eyes I can see all possibilities—Samantha and Joshua.

—LENORE WEISS BAIGELMAN

Contents

Preface

Every space has the potential to meet your needs. Whether you are thinking about altering one room in an existing home, building an addition, or shaping a dream home, this book is for you. It will help architects and designers uncover creative ideas for crafting supportive environments and help homeowners select a variety of templates from which they can formulate their plans. In the following pages professionals and novices alike will learn how to use feng shui principles to bring out the full potential of their residential spaces.

Countless books tell you how much a fireplace or hot tub will add to the value of a house, and armloads of magazines depict the latest trends and fashions. You can find books that describe in real estate terms how much you should pay for this feature or for that amount of square footage. Dozens of articles offer advice about hiring contractors, choosing the latest building products, and working with currently popular floor plans. However, few tell us how to shape a space to meet deep personal needs. *Feng Shui Principles for Building and Remodeling* offers concrete practical advice to those in the process of building, selecting, renovating, or revamping a home.

In the last few years a huge amount of information on feng shui has been poured into the public consciousness. The stories that have filled books and magazines are mostly anecdotal, with the lion's share making feng shui seem as if it were an esoteric or even occult phenomenon. Many who write about feng shui imply that the suggested feng shui applications will produce "luck." We believe that portraying feng shui as a form of magic minimizes and discredits it. We take a different approach. In fact our approach, the pyramid school of feng shui, a contemporary interdisciplinary version of an ancient Chinese practice, uses biology, physics, psychology, architecture, cultural anthropology, and other fields of study to explain how human beings filter information and how our physical environment can either support or thwart our deepest needs and desires.

"The control of man's environment will strengthen his health and physical fiber; man was born to be healthy. He is not born lazy, but becomes so from the frustration of being punished for his motions...."

R. BUCKMINSTER FULLER,
architect, engineer

The field of feng shui holds that our lives are influenced not only by chance—our unique combination of genetic potential and geographical and historical placement—and other people, but also by our environment. The floor plan of a home forces us into patterns that may or may not be beneficial. When the blueprint is correlated to our personal goals and proclivities, our ability to achieve our life's desires is enhanced. Yet we may not be consciously aware of which elements and conditions in our surroundings feel good and which feel bad. Why, for example, do rooms at right angles from each other encourage a more nurturing intimacy than those positioned directly across a hallway? The configuration of space dramatically affects how our lives unfold. It is the goal of pyramid feng shui to unearth the underlying reasons for the "good luck" that seems to come to us in some spaces and not in others.

Pyramid feng shui has codified the human response systems into a collection of principles. When you integrate these principles into your building and remodeling plans, a whole new set of options opens up for you. Without spending a dime more for new construction, renovation, or remodeling, you can create not just the house of your dreams but a home that encourages your personal dreams to materialize.

This book does not, however, dictate specific architecture, decorating styles, or aesthetic preferences. Pyramid feng shui goes beyond anecdotal and intuitive feng shui traditions to the core principles that can be applied to any style of architecture or interior design. By stripping away cultural biases and extracting universal truths, pyramid feng shui is able to produce plans that fit with Western building styles, suit contemporary life, and support specific individualized needs. In pyramid feng shui *you* are the most important ingredient. It is your requirements that dictate how your home should be configured. While taste, style, and architectural preferences are important, we are concerned with the patterns of living and the patterns of behavior that a home drives its occupants to experience.

The relationship between people and their living spaces is, of course, complex. If our living spaces are to remain beneficial over time, they must be able to adapt to our changing needs. They also need to accommodate various family configurations, from the traditional nuclear family to empty nesters with visiting children, singles, groups of unrelated adults, blended families, single-parent families, and reunited nesters. The more specifically your home answers all your needs, the more it will optimize a general sense of contentment for everyone living under your roof.

Whether you are a professional helping clients realize their dreams or one of the dreamers hoping to fulfill your desires, this book offers inspiration as well as pragmatic, inspirational housing templates. It is with a great deal of joy that we present these ideas. We envision our ideas as the yarn from which you can weave a cloak called home.

Part I

Tools for Personal Assessment

1

What Feng Shui Is and Why It Matters

If you have ever gasped with delight in response to an awe-inspiring scene, you have experienced a physical response to space. If you have ever felt uncomfortable or restless upon entering a place, you know what a negative reaction to an environment feels like. Because we tend to be more aware of extreme feelings, we often miss the emotional nuances that we continuously experience in reaction to our physical surroundings. Yet these nuances add up to a significant overall effect that any environment has on us. We react to place biologically, culturally, and personally in complex ways of which we are often unaware. Feng shui matters because it provides facts that help explain why we react the way we do to place.

Feng shui is a Chinese discipline developed thousands of years ago. Traditional feng shui incorporates beliefs and thought patterns that are specific to Chinese culture, and this may be why it has taken the Western world so long to see how its precepts might help us understand the intricacies of our responses to our surroundings. Perhaps because we now spend so much energy seeking ways to reach our peak potential and contentment, the West finally seems open to what feng shui can tell us. Pyramid feng shui, the school of feng shui on which this book is based, extracts the universal core concepts from this ancient discipline and shows how they can be applied in ways that are culturally acceptable in the West as well as the East. In other words, you don't have to have a home influenced by Asian traditions to benefit from feng shui.

Pyramid feng shui builds on the foundations of many disciplines, from biology to cultural anthropology to psychology. It takes into account the unique patterns of living of the individuals and groups who occupy a home. It helps us understand the laws of nature and how we can translate them with enough flexibility to accommodate our multifaceted needs and fulfill our diverse dreams. Throughout this book we will show you how some traditional feng shui principles, often viewed as mystical and unassailable, are in fact validated by current social and scientific data.

"Fill a room of your own with a piece of your heart, a passion for what is next, a collection of beauty to nourish your soul."

TAMARA RAND,
poet

Humans are by nature complex, and our responses to our homes are no exception. Choosing a new home, refurbishing an existing one, or building from scratch is like selecting a mate. When building and remodeling decisions are made without a great deal of thought, the results can be unfulfilling at best, disastrous at worst. For example, bigger is not necessarily better, as evidenced by one client's desire to reduce the size of her kitchen. The fifteen-by-eighteen-foot kitchen is by today's standards ample, and in conceptualizing it the home owners believed they were constructing their dream kitchen. However, after using the space for a few years, reality set in. It was too large and what we call the "carrot effect" became evident. How many steps did it take to get a carrot out of the refrigerator, carry to the sink to peel, take to the cutting board to chop, dump into boiling water on the stove, and then finally place on the table? In this case it took a total of twenty-one steps—way too many. In other words, the kitchen didn't function efficiently for this solo cook's needs. We hope you will examine your own experiences with an eye to how your world could be improved if you choose to apply the principles of feng shui.

A Brief History of Feng Shui

The physical environment is so fundamental to our self-esteem, the way we act toward one another, and our physical health that it is amazing how long it has taken us to formulate a discipline to address this relationship—at least in the West. Although inquiry into how a physical environment impacts human experience is relatively new to contemporary social and physical sciences, it has been important to the Chinese for millennia in the form of feng shui. The Chinese words *feng shui* mean, respectively, "wind" and "water," which underscores the importance of nature's role in the outcome of our lives.

Feng shui's emergence can be traced all the way back to the Stone Age. When Paleolithic hunters and gatherers stopped depending solely on the bounty of nature and began to cultivate the land for survival, communities and habitats became permanent. The twenty- to fifty-member groups expanded into larger villages, towns, and cities. No longer was it necessary for everyone to be involved in the procurement of food, and as the number of occupations increased, so did the need to customize space. For example, the baker needed an oven and storage for firewood, the scribe a good work surface, and the temple priest ample gathering space. Diversity became the mother of customized housing.

Furthermore, permanent dwellings gave rise to a new interpretation of the notion of centrality. To support the human need for belonging, ancient cities typically had plazas or central public gathering spaces, as illustrated in Figure 1.1. These central places became the magnet toward which citizens would gravitate to see and be seen, to share news, and to socialize. Plazas can be compared to a home's gathering space. As shown in Figure 1.2, in homes, as in traditional cities, all roads should lead to the center—like veins to the human heart.

Using human conditions as a basis for feng shui's precepts and merging them with the Chinese principles of Tao, ying and yang, and chi, can create a coherent paradigm that is useful in supporting a great many of feng shui's ideas. Feng shui peers at the world through the eyes of these three great principles. Understanding these concepts will clarify a great many feng shui ideas.

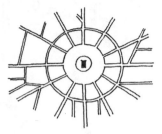

Figure 1.1 Be it a city or a home, as in a body all routes should lead to the heart.

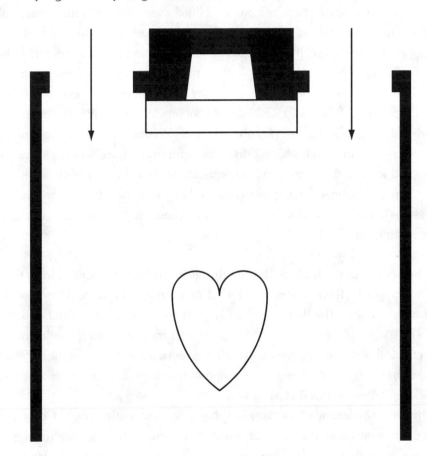

Figure 1.2 The heart of a home, like a plaza, becomes a home's focus when there are many passageways leading into it.

Tao: The Foundation of Connectedness

Tao ("dow") traditionally is thought of as the way things naturally are. It is a process rather than a thing. In the context of buildings, Tao sheds light on our need for centeredness. From the electron's flight around a nucleus to planets orbiting our sun, every system needs a central core that is both definable and vital to the system's functioning. Humans are pack animals, and our environments should make us feel that we are in a delineated, finite space with a clear-cut heart or center. Whether you live with five others or alone, your home and the broader environment in which you live needs a heart. In a town a square, park, or boulevard lined with cafés (or in the home, a place that allows residents to dine, relax, or socialize) is precisely what the Tao is all about.

Applied to how we live, the Tao draws us out of isolation into involvement or interaction. The Tao of home, then, emphasizes the importance of common spaces. A space where residents dine, socialize, and relax is the nucleus of a home, which is a physical expression of the Tao. Homes that do not provide any connective central areas engender a feeling of isolation in their inhabitants. Homes that separate the functions of dining, socializing, and relaxing discourage intimate associations and can ultimately produce a malaise that prods the inhabitants to fill much of their time with TV watching, working, or engaging in other solitary activities. If there are no visible connections to dining, socializing, and relaxing, a home will not have a recognizable, life-supporting heartbeat.

Literature and folklore often refer figuratively, as well as literally, to the life-supporting center of the home as the hearth. The word *hearth* is derived from the Old English *heorth*, which comes from the Indo-European *ker*, the ancient word for "fire." In the same way that the flames at the campsite were essential to the families and tribes who gathered there every night to protect themselves from the cold and predators, a central place around which to gather gives us a sense of bonding, safety, and mutual support. Figure 1.3 shows how to support this need for centeredness by removing walls to connect disparate spaces in a home.

Christopher Alexander's A *Pattern Language: Towns, Buildings, Construction* speaks definitively about the need for humans to circulate through the main gathering rooms as much as possible. Movement in a home needs to emanate from a central source, and patterns that divert occupants away from it are not inclined to be supportive to the inhabitants. Sarah Susanka, author of *The Not So Big House: A Blueprint for the Way We Really Live*, observes that guests in a home in which gathering rooms are not visually contiguous tend to congregate in a kitchen while the rooms built for socializing remain unused. Most of us have seen this happen; we seem to feel the need for a kitchen or hearth to socialize comfortably. Figure 1.4 illustrates a typi-

Figure 1.3 Notice how removal of walls in (a) connects the different areas of this home so that the Tao is more fully realized in (b).

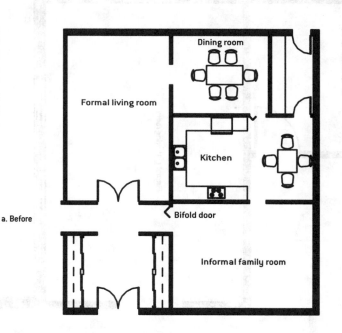

a. Before

This plan represents a portion of a typically traditional residential layout with self-contained rooms, each separated from the other and functioning somewhat independently.

The separation between the dining and living rooms has been removed to allow for greater ease of flow and better dining expansion and flexibility.

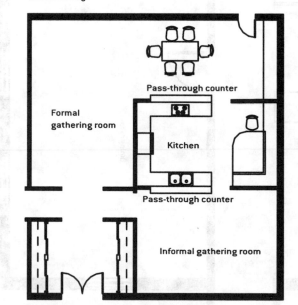

b. After

Doors in the hallway have been removed to further strengthen the visual continuity among functions.

The separate pantry area has been opened up to the dining area, with storage being accommodated by built-in furniture.

The wall between the kitchen and dining areas has been removed to allow for transparency at this location.

A cozy banquette or window seat could take the place of open kitchen seating, which would be duplicated with the opening to the dining area. Creating small, snug areas within larger open areas also helps create some balance by adding a yin element to an otherwise very yang space.

The wall between the kitchen and informal gathering room has been removed so that an opening exists between these areas.

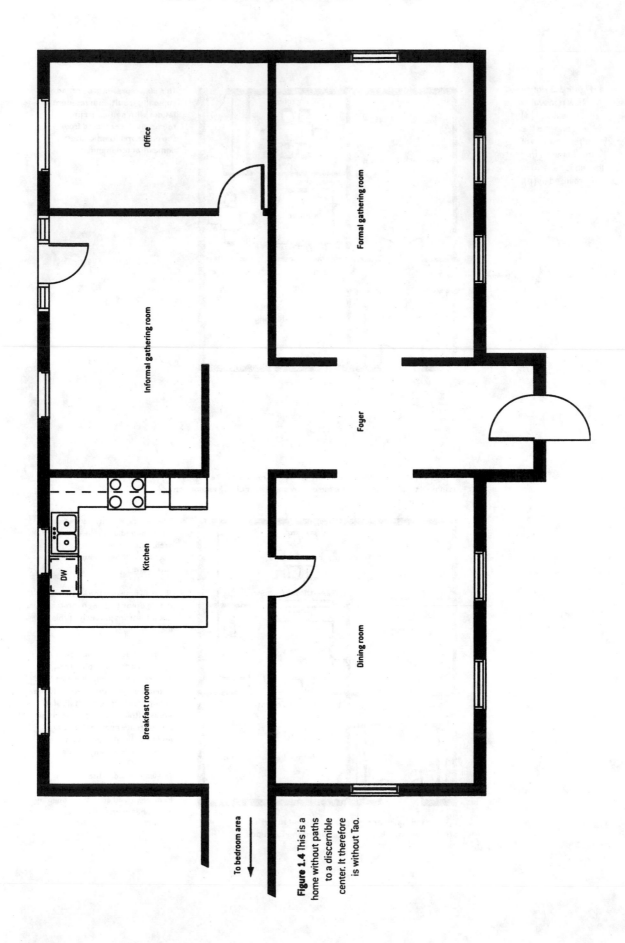

Office

Formal gathering room

Informal gathering room

Foyer

Kitchen

DW

Breakfast room

Dining room

To bedroom area

Figure 1.4 This is a home without paths to a discernible center. It therefore is without Tao.

cal plan that is the antithesis of this notion and therefore an example of what not to build.

Compare the feng shui–sensitive pattern of Tao as shown in Figure 1.5 with floor plans that tend to ignore the rooms' relationships to one another. Some floor plans have occupants pass existing gathering spaces to reach another. Every unused gathering space dissipates a home's cohesiveness, at great expense. One of the first decisions to make is how many gathering spaces are actually necessary. Consider how all rooms in Figures 1.5 and 1.6 flow toward the home's heart, making these plans that emphasize the Tao.

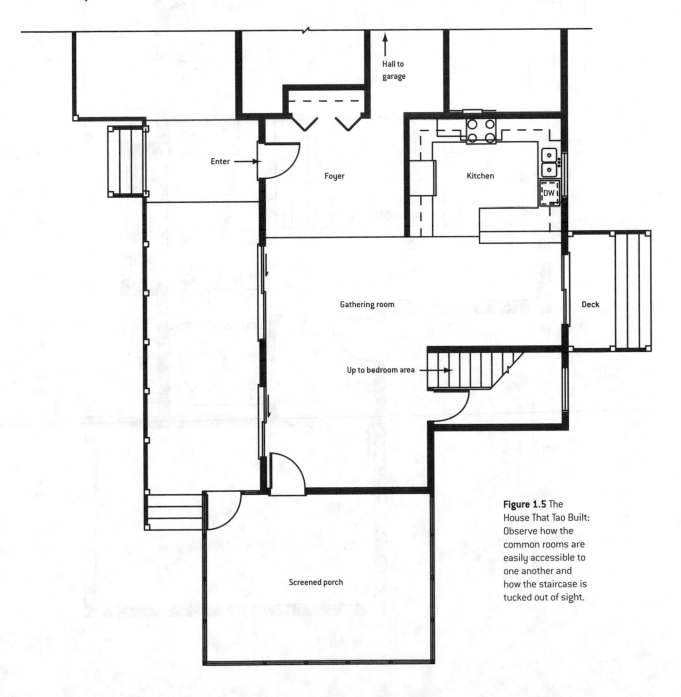

Figure 1.5 The House That Tao Built: Observe how the common rooms are easily accessible to one another and how the staircase is tucked out of sight.

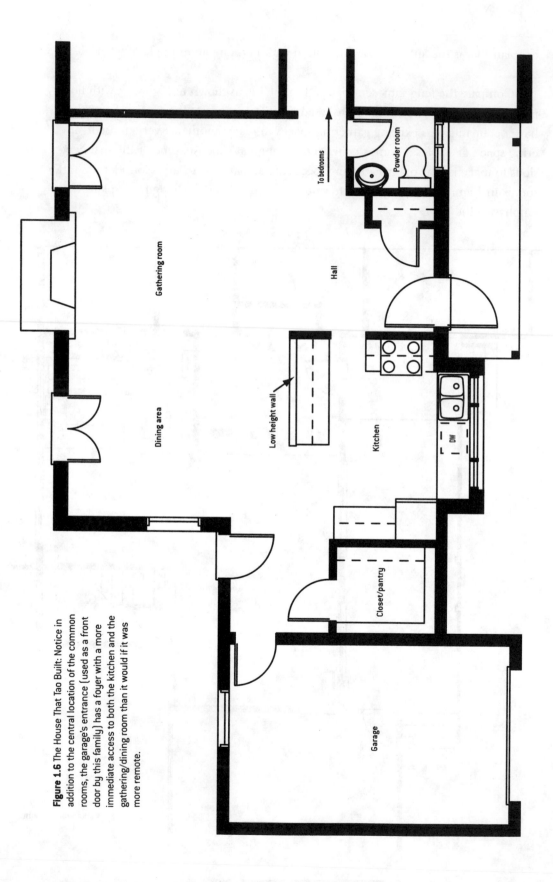

Figure 1.6 The House That Tao Built: Notice in addition to the central location of the common rooms, the garage's entrance (used as a front door by this family) has a foyer with a more immediate access to both the kitchen and the gathering/dining room than it would if it was more remote.

One more concept inherent in Tao that is important to consider in building and remodeling is order. Nature is highly organized. The growth of a seed is orderly and predictable, perfectly serving the need to produce an adult plant. Your home should be orderly too and should serve your own needs. A home that serves your personal needs is serving your personal Tao. Think of how unsettling it feels to enter a home through a space that is disorderly. In general, you can predict that the entryway to a home needs to provide for the appropriate storage of coats, shoes, and car keys as well as a convenient place for packages, mail, or reminders. To customize the entrance so it serves your personal Tao, figure out what you habitually do after crossing the threshold of your home.

A garage entrance that propels family members through the laundry, utility, or storage rooms before connecting them with the home's heart will make the initial Tao, or experience of home, unsettling. Chapter 5, "Entrances," and Chapter 10, "Remedies for Clutter," will discuss this in detail.

Yin and Yang: The Foundation of Balance

In *The Biology of Violence*, Debra Niehoff explains that sociopaths suffer from an underreactive autonomic nervous system while victims of post-traumatic stress syndrome suffer from an overreactive one. Too much or too little appears to be equally harmful. Being in balance is a preferred state for almost everything, and *yin* and *yang* are words that describe the extremes that in combination produce balance.

When in a yin state a person's focus is within. Yin environments support relaxing, thinking, introspection, and self-care. Quintessential yin can be exemplified by the way we experience a visit to a traditional museum. The atmosphere of cool, silent, and dimly lit rooms that are empty save for their artwork will inspire awe and put us into a contemplative state. This condition enables us to get in touch with the experience without feeling seduced to communicate our reaction to it. Yin conditions allow absorption, and in that way yin is very much like breathing in air.

Conversely, being in a yang state means overtly responding to outside stimuli and being in the frame of mind to interact with others. Yang conditions provoke active responses. Science museums for children are deliberately set up with yang conditions such as interactive displays to match the predominantly yang state of childhood. A space that encourages you to relate in a social or interactive way is yang. Yang spaces make it comfortable to initiate interaction and communication.

Yin and yang can influence how people will act inside a space. Consider the following list of possible yin and yang choices and use them appropriately.

ARCHITECTURAL YIN OR YANG

Yin	Yang
Small reading alcove	Large great room
Furniture placed against a solid wall	Free-standing furniture
Fireplace	Window with depth view
Low or partially lowered ceilings	High ceilings, skylights
Built-in upholstered seating (banquette)	Movable furniture
Cushioned carpeting	Hard-surfaced flooring (ceramic, stone tile, wood, or bamboo)
Solids or materials without patterns	Complex patterns, highly detailed or roughly textured surfaces (see Figure 1.7)
Specific and contrasting lighting, like a night sky	Overall intense lighting, like a sunny day

Certain areas serve the inhabitants better when they lean more toward either yin or yang, depending on their function or use. Before you decide to make changes to add more yin or more yang, however, consider whether the general rule applies to you; you may find that you have your own reasons for choosing either yin or yang for a room. We have categorized dining rooms as yang spaces because we believe that most of us favor lively conversation during mealtime. However, a newly married couple may want to extend the atmosphere of their honeymoon, with its deliciously mellow

Figure 1.7 Complex or highly detailed surfaces are yang (a), while solid surfaces or those without patterns are yin (b).

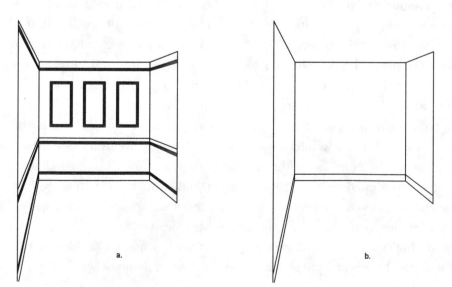

a.

b.

LIKELY YIN OR YANG SPACES

Likely Yin Spaces	**Likely Yang Spaces**
Bathrooms	Gathering rooms
Bedrooms	Kitchen
Library	Dining area
Home offices for concentration	Home offices for communication, hobby or game rooms

---

candlelit dining, when the whole world felt as remote as the island they vacationed on. Using yin conditions would do much to replicate that mood.

A home's threshold needs a mixture of yin and yang because the threshold should provide time for personal adjustment (yin) and then stimulate the person to proceed (yang).

Determine a room's overall tone by assessing the presence of the conditions in the following table; then adjust those conditions accordingly to create either a yin or a yang atmosphere for each of your rooms.

CONDITIONS THAT CAN CREATE A YIN OR A YANG ATMOSPHERE

What Contributes to a Yin Atmosphere

Curved, undulating paths

Low light or pools of light

Deeper or muted colors

Flooring that muffles sounds

Low level of ambient sounds

Proportionately intense aromatics

Textures that are smooth and soothing to touch

What Contributes to a Yang Atmosphere

Straight paths

Intense and overall bright lighting

Brighter, more primary colors

Hard flooring that resounds with footsteps

Intermittent sounds with distinct tones

Clean, clear aromatics

Textures that stimulate and arouse feelings

Chi: The Foundation of Sensorial Experiences

Chi is often mistakenly portrayed as a separate entity. You may have heard chi described as if it moved around a house, vaulted out a window, or as something potentially bad. Descriptions like these only make chi impossible to understand. Therefore, pyramid feng shui defines chi as the composite of human sensorial experience including sight, sound, smell, touch, and the capacity for mobility. Chi acts as the filter through which we take in information from the physical world. Without seeing, hearing, smelling, touching, and being able to negotiate through a space, we would have no information about our surroundings. Our chi capacity allows us to experience our world, a veritable sensorial orchestra in which all living creatures participate.

The way our five senses take in information from the environment plays a huge role in our experience of place. In nature, elements that stimulate all our senses are omnipresent. Just walk outside your front door. You are sure to see some sort of vegetation, hear intermittent sounds, feel a breeze or the warmth of the sun on your skin, smell a flower or the damp earth, and observe the movement of a critter or a plant's leaves. Nature is the elixir that vitalizes us. As we move inside, we miss many of nature's sensorial messages. Without them, a space feels "dead" and sterile. Yet we rarely build our homes with our needs for scent or movement in mind. How many times have you entered a space that was planned without consideration to sound or variety of texture? For example, the choice of flooring material can affect a family's sense of fellowship by allowing members' footsteps to be heard; if a home is completely carpeted, family members' locations may be obscured. My mother would catch my father cheating on his diet by the click of the magnetic latch on the cupboard storing his favorite chocolates. Choosing a touch-latch, bifold, or traditional knob for a door is not only a cost or aesthetic consideration; the sounds they make can indicate an occupant's whereabouts. While these considerations may seem minute compared to planning the size and placement of rooms, it is the life-sustaining elements of the materials, flooring, style of windows, and other elements like these that give spaces charisma.

All aspects of chi must be taken into consideration if a space is to furnish its occupants with a satisfying human experience. With that in mind, let's review the fundamentals of the five sensorial experiences of chi.

Sight

Have you ever considered why grass is green, the sky is blue, and the sun appears yellow? If we look at which objects in nature are the same colors, we can see that certain colors express a particular spirit of other phenomenon. For example, most of the vegetation on this planet is green. Green is the color of chlorophyll, the substance that

NATURE'S USE OF COLORS AND THEIR UNDERLYING EMOTIONAL MESSAGES

Color	Use in Nature	Emotional Message
Red	Fire	Invites action, instigates movement
Red	Blossoms	Attracts attention
Yellow	Sun	Illuminates, clarifies, cleanses
Yellow	Plants ready for harvest	At peak of fertility, at the brink of decay
Blue	Sky	Inspires contemplation
Blue	Water	Stimulates self-exploration or exploring limits
Green	Plants	Evokes growth
Purple	Blooms	Aligned with exotic and unexplainable phenomena
White	Sand	Reflects great experience or self-attention
Black	Night, shadow	Inspires mystery, intrigue

permits growth, through photosynthesis. Therefore, green can comfortably be associated with vitality, growth, or change. Pyramid feng shui recognizes, therefore, that a color's hue expresses its personality. When we surround ourselves with a specific color, we are captured by its message. Indeed, it makes a difference in a kitchen whether you choose green or blue tiles. Choosing green subconsciously aligns a person with vegetation, a prime ingredient for health, while blue—a color rarely seen in foodstuff—resonates with introspection, which, for those who must be conscious of food choices, could be a better selection.

Sound

In nature objects in motion create sound. Even the wind finds a plethora of instruments on which to play a tune.

Mothers hum lullabies to soothe their infants. We utter an exclamation when a child tumbles and cries out in pain. Laughter spontaneously erupts when we are amused. A multitude of sounds, whether learned or not, burst forth from the depths of our humanity. Where there is activity there is sound. Because our homes have sound-reducing exterior walls, we must pay more attention to replicating the music of nature inside. When designing a home, consider how simple human actions can create a symphony of vocalizations.

SOUNDS AND THEIR UNDERLYING EMOTIONAL MESSAGES

Quality of Sound	What It Inspires	Some Suggested Sources
Occasional and staccato	Wake-up call, astonishes	Bell on door, hourly chime on clock
Consistent and ongoing	Safety	Ticking clock, footsteps
Spinning, slipping	Cocoons in concentration	Evenly flowing water
Fluttering, soothing	Emotional comfort	Material billowing in a breeze
Straining and stretching	Change and exploration	Sound of a door or window opening

Sounds, like colors, are associated with different characteristics or moods. The pounding crash of an ocean's wave, the mournful wail of a coyote's call, and the perky chirps of wrens evoke specific feelings. In space planning it is therefore imperative to consider the auditory interplay between the materials of a home and the occupants' movement. The above chart will give you some ideas about how sounds act on us.

Flooring is the most consistent sound producer in a home. The sound of footsteps on a surface is a home's life force. Even for those who live alone, the sounds of their own footsteps can be comforting. Installing a variety of flooring materials is one way to change the tune as you move from area to area.

On a recent visit to Bali, I rented a traditional pole house that in place of permanent walls had only woven rattan blinds that were rolled down at night or when it rained. Thus connected to nature's sounds, I rarely felt the need for a clock while living there. The roosters' crowing announced the sun's arrival, and at dusk when the sun set over the treetops the conversations among birds signaled the day's ending. Nature's vocal patterns became a rhythmic backdrop to the passage of time. Finally, as each day's light faded into the pale glow of moonlight, another symphony of sounds began. Crickets rubbed their legs together, owls' hoots pierced the night air, and the frogs' croaking added a drum beat to the mix. My clock never needed to be wound, for I was living with the natural sounds of time.

Spaces such as open courtyards, decks, or patios receive the innate benefit of nature's auditory stimulation all through the warm season—birdsong, the scampering of squirrels, the rustle of leaves, or the purposeful placing of the ever-popular wind chimes hung to catch the music of the breezes.

Touch

I hate wearing shoes. Ever since I was a child, I have felt more comfortable barefoot. When babies learn to walk, they are much steadier if they are able to use their toes to grip the ground. Feet are the body parts most consistently in physical contact with our surroundings.

Skin is the largest sensory organ. While this is not new or surprising to most of us, we usually don't select materials primarily for their tactile qualities. We tend to select materials for their color and pattern or their ease of care. Fine. However, building with materials based on their tactile quality will add an interaction between you and the environment otherwise absent. If you use a variety of tactile materials in a home, it ceases to be a mere showcase. It becomes more of an immersion, like a warm bath.

Focusing on the feel of architectural forms is not new, although hardly applied consistently enough. In his book *In the Nature of Materials, 1887–1941: The Buildings of Frank Lloyd Wright*, Henry-Russell Hitchcock describes the architect's belief that indigenous building materials and forms were key to the integrity of a structure. (In fact Wright himself selected the title for this book.) Wright remained true to this conviction when he built his prairie houses, which evoked the midwestern American prairie not only in their horizontal lines but also in their rich use of local materials. The warmth of wood and the undulating texture of clay in the brickwork contributed to a tactile quality that spoke strongly of the natural surroundings. Wright's use of honest indigenous materials made for strikingly comfortable and balanced living spaces that harmonized with the surrounding environment. There are many ways to bring more tactile sensations to your living space. The following lists will get you started.

SUGGESTIONS FOR TACTILE VARIETY IN A HOME

Light Switches
Flip
Turn
Slide
Punch
Clap (sound that can turn on a light)

Counter Surfaces
Smooth—natural stone, granite, wood,
    Corian, Formica, concrete
Grouted—tile, stone, metal
Pitted—alabaster, grainy wood, some tiles

Stairway Handrails
Wood, smooth or carved
Metal, thick or thin
Synthetic—composite materials

Flooring Materials
Various textures of carpets
Different patterns of wood
Tile in a variety of sizes and shapes
Natural stone pavers in different
    shapes or sizes

Door and Cabinet Handles
Round knobs that turn
Levers that can be pushed down
Fingertip-size pulls

The Finnish architect Alvar Aalto was, like Frank Lloyd Wright, well known for his consideration of the tactile quality of the environments and furniture he created. As an example, he responded to criticism of the discomfort of modern bent-metal chairs by developing new techniques to bend wood that allowed him to create furniture that was "warm to the touch and using a natural material." Aalto's creative use of materials and forms to enhance the feel of a space and his general attention to what the writer Sigfried Giedion called "the human side" of modern architecture has earned him a place among the most influential architects of the twentieth century.

In addition to experiencing textures, we feel temperatures, and your space should offer diversity there too. Remember, the more variety a space has, the more it springs to life. Have you ever rested your face against a cool windowpane? This glass membrane separating you from the elements serves tactile as well as thermal purposes. Window seats, like the one shown in Figure 1.8, can offer both.

Places to Consider for Window Seats
Kitchens
Bathrooms, so long as the toilet is in a separate room
Tucked-away places like stairway landings
Rooms with fireplaces

Figure 1.8 Window seats give occupants a variety of thermal experiences since glass is often the least insulated barrier between interior and exterior.

Who does not delight in feeling the breeze from an open window on the skin? When building or renovating, carefully consider the placement of air vents, windows, and doors for their thermal and tactile variety. Figure 1.9 shows window placement that helps this southern gathering space dissipate hot air.

Air movement should be integrated into a home's plan. Ceiling fans circulate the heat trapped at the highest point in a room throughout a space. Inside air movement, like a breeze outside, can make a warm day comfortable.

Scent

A bad smell is a turnoff just as a favored scent is an attraction. Realtors know that the aroma of apple pies or the scent of cider wafting from oven or stovetop can add to a potential buyer's positive association with a house. However, with the exception of cedar-lined closets, architects generally pay little attention to building scents into a home.

It was through their olfactory nerves that our prespecies ancestors filtered information from their surroundings. Without a keen ability to smell danger, be it a poisoned berry or a predator on the prowl, our primordial ancestors could not have survived. Just from the location of the nose on the face, you have to assume that its importance is central to our well-being.

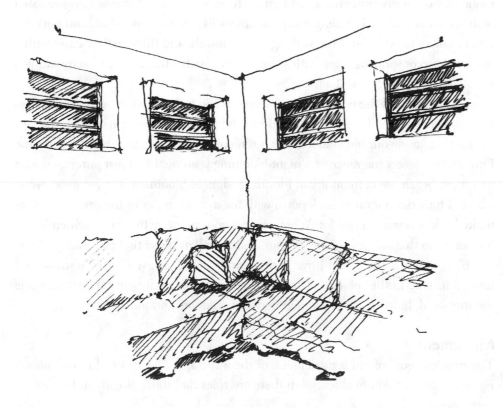

Figure 1.9
Clerestory windows that open can regulate thermal comfort because they allow naturally rising heat to escape. Further, they offer light without sacrificing wall space.

Why, then, are features that dispense scent summarily ignored? The main reason is that our awareness of an aroma remains with us for a very short period of time. An enzyme present inside the nose actually flushes out what we are smelling. We have all been repelled by a rotten odor or attracted by a sweet scent only to find ourselves unaware of the smell a short while later. We experience scents fleetingly. Therefore, transition areas are the ones that can best benefit most from having an integrated fragrance.

Transition Areas in Which to Infuse Scents
Exterior entrances
Thresholds of rooms
Hallways
Bathrooms
Stairways

Figure 1.10 A recessed outlet with a retractable grille can be a more aesthetic and sophisticated receptacle for a commercial plug-in scent dispenser.

Heat, air, and water all diffuse scents. You can dispense a scent continuously by using receptacles attached to lightbulbs and plug-in heat dispensers that run on electricity. Figure 1.10 shows an attractive way to install a plug-in scent dispenser, but you should also consider using a water feature to circulate fragrances into the air, a technique that often dispenses the scent farthest from the source. Materials impregnated with scents or materials with natural fragrances like cedar, pine, sisal, and cork are other choices to consider. Also washing linens, towels, and throw pillow cases with a fragrant soap or spraying them with scent can be an effective way of disseminating a variety of scents throughout a home.

Every scent has the potential to motivate us and influence our behavior, but you have to know what different scents evoke in the psyche to choose wisely for the particular room and your individual needs. I remember feeling captivated the first time I inhaled the sweet fragrance of a night-blooming jasmine. I had just purchased a lot in a small beachside community in Florida, and night-blooming jasmine grew everywhere. I took the fragrance back north with me as a reminder of the dream to eventually build a home on this lot. When you fill your home with scents, remember to include ones that are indigenous to your area as well as those that can transport you to a place you love. Now that I live in my Florida home, I have planted jasmine and trained its vine in the spindles of my front-step banister to dispense the scent inside the threshold, blurring the separation between outdoors and indoors.

Movement
The final category of chi is movement, or the way a space obliges us to move about. For instance, in traditional feng shui there are rules that stairs directly in line with a

SCENTS TO CHOOSE FOR PARTICULAR EFFECTS

Stimulation, Refreshment, and Energizing

Lemon balm	Tea tree
Rose	Clove
Jasmine	Grapefruit
Ginger	Bergamot
Laurel	Cardamom

Support, Unification, and Stability

Fennel	Vetiver
Lemon	Caraway
Sweet marjoram	Cedar wood
Coriander	Benzoin
Peppermint	

Clarity, Focus, and Concentration

Tea tree	Basil
Pine	Laurel
Eucalyptus	Thyme
Clary sage	Coriander
Marjoram	Lemon
Frankincense	Peppermint
Rosemary	Geranium

Emotional Connections and Compassion

Geranium	Cedar wood
Juniper berry	Ylang-ylang
Red thyme	Cardamom
Jasmine	Rose
Lavender	Patchouli
Ginger	Fennel

Optimism for Growth and Change, Leadership, and the Ability to Thrive Under Pressure

Bergamot	Ginger
Chamomile	Eucalyptus
Peppermint	Orange
Grapefruit	

front entrance produce negative chi and that a bathroom next to a front door initiates financial loss. These rules are organized around the principle that chi is a separate entity and can do things like rush upstairs, be associated with money, or perpetrate loss.

Pyramid feng shui has more rational answers. Stairs near the front door are potential detractors from a home's common areas. Since bedrooms are often located on the second floor and since the human eye sees diagonal lines before horizontal or vertical ones upon entering, our attention is drawn to our private space rather than the common ones. There is no justification in our minds for associating money with chi, and so pyramid feng shui says that bathrooms near the front door may or may not be appropriate.

The concept of movement includes seeing other objects move. In nature, breezes shift vegetation, animals scurry, the sun and moon travel across the sky, clouds drift, and humans and pets are often in motion. We expect to view our world in flux.

Sheer curtains moved by breezes in open windows can be a seasonal solution as can the placement of windows to stimulate cross-ventilation that brings nature's movement inside. If a home has a forced-air heating and cooling system, the air ducts can be directed at mobiles and other lightweight materials. Ceiling fans to engage kinetic sculptures are another way to incorporate movement inside.

Be sure to give consideration to the flow to and around furniture. A room's spaciousness is judged by how freely both our feet and our eyes can move about. Remember that every room has to serve a given number of people. To do so well, it has to have a certain number of square feet of space per person. Each culture has standards for personal spatial comfort. For example, England's royal family needs more space than commoners do because it is considered intrusive to sit close to the queen or other royals. On the contrary, you might insult an Italian family if you moved a chair away from them before sitting to converse. The amount of personal space needed varies according to each individual's age, level and type of activity, and culture.

Feng shui speaks to the human capacity to inculcate experience. When all of our senses are stimulated, we feel more fully alive and vital, and as a result we are more content. Pyramid feng shui teaches us to build experiences that serve people, not just the prevailing aesthetics or fashion *d'jour*.

2

Remodel, Buy, or Build?

Why do our ideas of a dream house sometimes fail to deliver their promise? The answer is that we usually yield to conventional wisdom rather than evaluate and try to answer our own unique needs. Maybe we opt for what everyone declares "in" and "chic." Or we decide our home should reflect our financial stature—even if it doesn't suit our lifestyle. Often we plan for a future resale rather than plan a space that will serve us, the home's current inhabitants. The formal dining room is a good example of an amenity we often think we need when in reality we don't. A phrase like "elegant formal dining room" may look good in a real estate ad, but a room dedicated solely to entertaining a dozen or more people now and then might be as practical as buying and maintaining a car used only on national holidays. That space might better serve as a library or home office.

A home should serve the family's goals as well as each individual's needs. Suppose you agree that the highest goal of a home is to provide a nest that stands secure no matter what life throws your way, as well as acting as a forum from which each individual can draw strength to tackle life's requirements. This makes it important for a home to provide an impenetrable psychological boundary and give each family member space to develop self-confidence to go forth into the world. These needs can be translated into the physical environment. When a space does not have the specificity that individual family members require, like no appropriate homework space for school-aged children or no place for a stressed working adult to decompress, then the individual is forced to subjugate his or her needs because of what the physical space lacks. Moreover, if a space has only one gathering room and that room is typically used for TV watching, how can the home provide a safe haven for family members to express their feelings and learn how to interact emotionally with others?

Only you can develop the list of home characteristics that dovetails specifically with your family's needs. Remember to consider the specific needs of each individual as well as the group.

> *"The reality of the building consisted not of the four walls and the roof but of the space within."*
>
> LAO-TZU,
> *ancient philosopher*

Individual Needs	Remodel: Present House Has Space	Add On: There Is Land Available	Better to Buy or Build Anew
Wife's Needs			
Office away from household activity	x		
Exercise room		x	
Husband's Needs			
Own bathroom			x
Room to watch sports in	x		
Hobby/activity center			x
Family Needs			
Place for intimacy other than bedroom	x		
Room for two adults during food preparation		x	

A house assessment might look something like this. In this case, it appears that with modifications the present home could support both the individual and joint requirements of the family.

What Does Your Home Do for You, and What Do You Need?

It is the inability to integrate personal needs into workable floor plans that often translates dreams into screams and makes you start to think the only alternative is to move. Before making any drastic decisions, however, consider exactly how your home is and is not serving you and your family. Try to block out distracting thoughts like "Our house is so much smaller than everyone else's" and "If only we had a state-of-the-art kitchen like Dan and Susan's" and "We'll never be able to sell this place unless we add a bathroom." It may seem important to have as nice a house as your friends and neighbors, and it may seem astute and financially responsible to plan so you get the greatest possible profit from what may be your biggest investment. But pyramind feng shui says that the most important factor to consider in evaluating whether a home is right for you is whether it contributes to a life of contentment and helps you achieve your dreams. To make an informed decision about whether you need to and want to remodel your existing home or find a new one, answer the following questions. As explained in Chapter 1, a home can satisfy all kinds of needs that housing is not ordinarily thought to satisfy, beginning with the deep-seated need for a life of contentment.

In the last chapter we covered the three main underpinnings of feng shui. Using this information, analyze your housing needs based on the questions below. Take this test to evaluate how appropriately your spaces fulfill their highest and best expression of Tao, yin/yang, and chi. The more "yes" answers to the questions, the better the space fulfills feng shui's basic philosophies.

Tao Considerations

1. Do visitors to your home know it is yours before they enter?
2. Is the most frequently used entrance modified to accommodate each inhabitant's most pressing needs?
3. Do you pass the most frequently used gathering space when entering your home?
4. Do you pass the most frequently used gathering space when exiting the kitchen or dining area?
5. Do you pass the most frequently used gathering space when exiting the bedroom area?
6. Can you observe neighborhood activity from at least two frequently used locations?
7. Is there at least one important or strong architectural feature in each gathering space? (For example, is there a fireplace in a main gathering space?)

Yin/Yang Considerations

1. Is tranquility a benefit you desire from your home and, if so, are there curved pathways leading to entrance doors and from room to room?
2. If you would benefit from being energized as you return home, can you see either red, green, or yellow objects or vegetation near your entrance?
3. Are there rooms with significantly low levels of general lighting in which you can read or relax in?
4. Are there rooms in which you feel pleasantly cocooned and private?
5. Are there opportunities for right-angle seating in gathering spaces?
6. If you use your kitchen for a morning pick-me-up, such as breakfast or reading the newspaper, does it have an east-facing window?
7. If you enjoy entertaining, does your home seem to be a good forum for parties?

Chi Considerations

1. Can you hear other family members' movements even when they are not in the same room?
2. Can you pass into another room whose colors or textures are substantially different from the room exited?
3. Independent of cooking odors, can you identify a room in your home by scent while blindfolded?
4. Can you proceed to the main seating in your gathering space without circumventing another piece of furniture?
5. Can you hear at least two sounds in your home other than those generated by humans?
6. Are there at least three substantially differently textured types of seating throughout your home?
7. Can you feel or see the effects of a breeze anywhere in your home?

In the best of all possible scenarios you should have few "no" answers to these questions. If there are some, you will find ways to mitigate them in this book. In most cases, we have found that remodeling is an economical remedy. However, if you find that revamping a home becomes too costly or requires nothing short of Houdini's magic, then perhaps building anew is in order.

Do You Need to Make a Move?

If you have determined that, in fact, your residence is not your dream home, you can choose to remodel without making changes to the exterior walls, build an addition that would add more square footage by extending the exterior footprint (building beyond the existing foundation and walls), build from scratch, or buy an existing home. The needs that you identified in the preceding quiz may give you some ideas about which route you want to take. If you're still not sure whether you need to move or can make some kind of adjustments to your present home, the upcoming questions about your home's location might help.

When I was looking for my first home, I established two tough criteria. The first was to find an affordable home—it had to be below the current market price in my chosen location. Second, I had to have complete and uncompromised privacy. I told real estate agents that I had to be able to walk out my front door naked and not get arrested. I did find a primitive structure that I ended up transforming into my dream palace. What I failed to consider, though, was how my home's location would affect my life. Even though I am by nature friendly and outgoing, it took me four years to find a network of people I could relate to. My community had no centers, places of learning, or a downtown area to support a heart, so I met my neighbors in a hit-or-miss way. Ultimately I found that meeting the requirements of the actual space was almost less important than the context in which the home existed.

With that in mind, the first step is always to ascertain the kind of community and neighborhood in which you will thrive. The following quiz will help you uncover your primary requirements for community. You may find that your present neighborhood satisfies your criteria, in which case you might look for another home very close by or add to your current home rather than seek another location. In any case, remember community is the springboard for all of the experiences you have in your home. Be diligent in ascertaining your needs.

Assessing the Importance of Community

Use the following questions to assess how important these characteristics are to you (choose all of the answers that apply to you). Then use this list to rate communities you are considering and compare them with the present location.

1. What convenience do I want most in a neighborhood?
   a. shopping nearby
   b. recreational activities nearby
   c. walking distance or a short driving distance from friends and family
   d. schools
   e. parks/open spaces
   f. easy access to work by car or public transportation

2. What type of neighborhood makes me feel most content?
   a. one that offers seclusion and privacy
   b. one that is centrally located and in the thick of things
   c. one that offers a little of both in a suburban setting
   d. one that has social status in the community

3. Which level of interaction with neighbors does my family enjoy?
   a. ongoing socializing
   b. mutual support without in-your-face friendliness
   c. privacy without any pressure to interact socially at all

4. What type of neighborhood makeup do I prefer?
   a. mixed age groups
   b. families with children

    c. retirees

    d. mixed cultural groups

    e. mixed economic makeup

5. Which transportation options do we need?
   a. good roadways
   b. easy access to hired transport (taxi, on-call shuttle, etc.)
   c. public surface transportation
   d. fast underground or surface public transportation
   e. easy walks (with safe sidewalks) to conveniences
   f. bicycle paths
   g. hiking trails and footpaths

6. Which facilities and amenities would I like to have within a ten-minute drive or walk?
   a. open space
   b. schools or other institutions of learning
   c. community centers such as a YMCA, community pools, parks, and teen centers
   d. food shopping
   e. sport activity centers
   f. house of worship
   g. golf courses, tennis courts
   h. workplace
   i. community garden plots
   j. cultural centers

7. Which of the following amenities and facilities would I like to have within a thirty-minute drive?
   a. park with facilities for children
   b. park with tennis, jogging paths, or walking trails
   c. wooded trails for horseback riding, biking, or walking
   d. appropriate bike-riding pathways
   e. golf or year-round racquetball or tennis facilities
   f. body of water for swimming, boating, fishing
   g. post office
   h. convenient food shopping

Now evaluate your current neighborhood. Does it meet these needs? If it has fewer than half of the features you consider important, you may consider moving. When you seek a new community or neighborhood, keep these answers as a guide.

If you are satisfied with your location but not your home, should you move or remodel? First check the following list.

You Might Want to Leave Your Existing Structure When . . .
- Family size expands or shrinks
- Your home has poor accessibility for changing physical needs
- The school system, transportation, or proximity to your workplace is inadequate for your current needs
- A remodeling or addition would make the home priced too high for its location
- The lot is too small to accommodate the extra square footage you desire
- An environmental condition threatens or is affecting a family member
- The neighborhood does not warrant adding value to your home

You can seek an expert's advice on whether, from an architectural standpoint, your current needs can be met in your existing home, whether the improvements would make practical and economic sense, and whether they could be made within the confines of local building codes/zoning ordinances. These are practical issues, but there are many intangible personal issues to address as well. Feng shui and its vocabulary of space can help you examine your situation more comprehensively. First of all, if you're thinking of building an addition to your home, you need to determine whether you really need more floor space or whether current spaces are just not proportioned or allocated in a way that supports your personal lifestyle.

Do You Really Need More Space or Just a Reallocation of the Space You Have?

Here's a fairly typical scenario. A family requests an addition of a family room when a formal living room and a rarely used dining room already exist. In spite of the obvious efficacy of using the preexisting space to fulfill family needs, many homeowners cite the conventional real estate wisdom that a formal living room and dining room should be preserved solely to maintain resale value. Well, it seems to us that it is a very expensive proposition to maintain five hundred square feet of space or more for the purpose of getting a higher price in the future. What if the family lives there for fifteen years? In the interim, they may find themselves crammed into smaller informal living areas that are inadequate for their needs.

In this case there is little doubt that changes should be made, but adding on to a house that already has large rooms gathering dust may not be the wisest choice. Besides the money, time, and effort that an addition will cost (and the higher resale price you'll feel you have to get to recoup those expenses), traditional feng shui tells us that it is costly to leave existing spaces unused. In this case the cost is not only financial but physical. Feng shui teaches us that a house, like our personal talents, should be used to the fullest. Like unused talent, unused space is not only a waste but can also disrupt the harmony that exists when all parts of a system operate at their best. In contrast, extraneous spaces—rooms not used regularly and in meaningful ways—drain us because they are a metaphor for failing to tap our own potential.

Sarah Susanka, a well-known architect from Minnesota, explains in *The Not So Big House* how emotionally satisfying homes can be created by rethinking the quality rather than simply the quantity of space. Including details that delight the senses is one way, and so are floor plans that fit modern living patterns.

We couldn't agree more! Many of us are trying to live twenty-first-century lives in homes whose architectural styles were developed early in the twentieth century or even earlier. The large-screen TVs, computer setups, and elaborate audio systems of today have replaced the conversation and card games that were the main source of home entertainment decades ago, but we often still live in homes with small parlor-style gathering spaces. Or we have kitchens that sequester the cook, who today would much rather stay at the party while preparing a meal for guests. No wonder "great rooms" and open kitchens have become so popular—they facilitate our increasingly informal living style.

So, if you are lucky enough to live in an older house with little-used existing spaces, consider reallocating space to serve present needs before considering an addition. Although it does include an addition, Figure 2.1 shows how one family reallocated unused space (a formal dining room) to meet a greater need. The home was a traditional suburban colonial, and the family wanted a larger kitchen but also a library/study close by so the mother could help with homework while she cooked. As you can see, although task-oriented, this plan does not compromise privacy, and the fact that the mother doesn't have to run to another part of the home every time one of her children needs help makes this configuration ideal. When we analyzed the existing spaces, it quickly became clear that the formal dining room next to the kitchen was rarely used as intended. In fact, in this warm, relaxed family the need for a separate, formal dining room did not exist at all, so it was converted into a study. To accommodate frequent guests, an addition was created for the kitchen with a larger and better-functioning cooking space that opened to an informal dining area that could

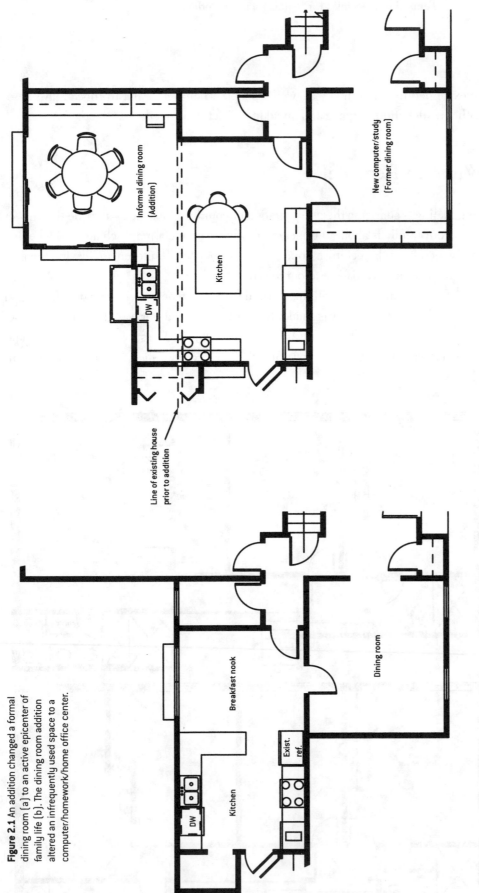

Figure 2.1 An addition changed a formal dining room (a) to an active epicenter of family life (b). The dining room addition altered an infrequently used space to a computer/homework/home office center.

Line of existing house prior to addition

Informal dining room (Addition)

Kitchen

DW

New computer/study (Former dining room)

b. After

Breakfast nook

Kitchen

DW

Exist. ref.

Dining room

a. Before

be expanded to seat as many as twenty people when necessary. In this family's case, both a reallocation of space and an addition met their needs.

When to Remodel

Remodeling—changing the configuration of your interior space—may be the answer when your family is about to undergo or has undergone a major change. Maybe one family member is launching a home-based business, the children are leaving the nest for college, or a third baby is about to arrive.

A friend of mine lived with his son and married a woman with two daughters, and his three-bedroom home was suddenly too small. He did not want to leave his home, so he converted three bedrooms into four, probably at a cost of what movers would have charged him. Figure 2.2 shows how this was accomplished without putting on an addition.

Figure 2.2 By converting three bedrooms (a) to four (b), a growing family was able to remain in its current house.

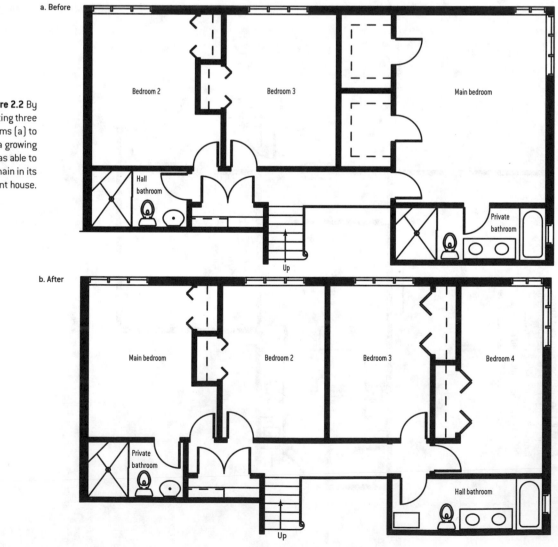

If you have unused rooms that cannot simply be reallocated for a new use, perhaps they can be converted easily through remodeling. The following sections will help you assess whether a present room is serving an appropriate function.

Is the Dining Room in Use Less than Once Every Two Weeks?

While it is absolutely necessary to be able to prepare a potential space for the occasional large group, it is an expensive and totally superfluous luxury to leave an infrequently used room alone when space is in short supply. But if you eliminate the dining room, what in the world will you do with the dining room set, curio cabinet, and eight chairs? Think of a grand old library with a large table used for things other than dining. In most cases a dining table can be moved to another space and used for a multitude of tasks. If your table is square, oval, or rectangular, consider pushing it against a wall to provide a practical surface on which family members can engage in daily amusements or study. If the table is round, move it into a corner as with a game table and free up floor space for alternative uses.

Sometimes freeing up space for other purposes can be as simple as pushing out a wall and creating a dining niche. Figure 2.3 shows one way to create a dining niche out of a porch area, freeing up the planned dining area for other uses.

Do You Have a Guest Room That Is Used Less than Once a Month?

Certainly most of us want to accommodate visiting friends and relatives comfortably, but you may not need a whole separate room for this. Before I added a sleeping loft,

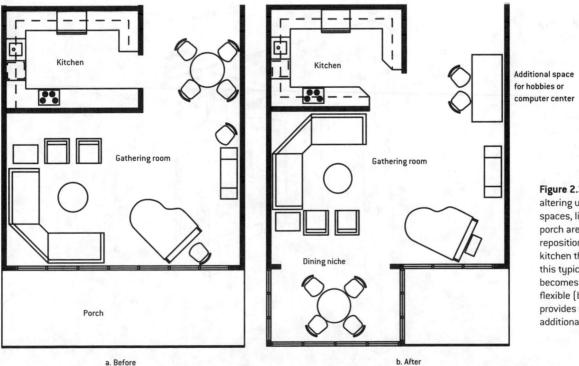

Additional space for hobbies or computer center

Kitchen

Gathering room

Dining niche

Kitchen

Gathering room

Porch

a. Before

b. After

Figure 2.3 By altering underused spaces, like the porch area (a), and repositioning the kitchen threshold, this typical layout becomes more flexible (b) and provides space for additional activities.

I would relinquish my bedroom to guests. A loft is perfect for young and physically fit visitors. When the existing roof structure can be reframed correctly, a part of the ceiling can be removed to gain enough height for a loft. If the area underneath is used as seating space, the underside of the loft can be comfortably used with lower ceiling heights.

The intimate, safe, cozy feel of a space under a loft area is yin, while the area unencumbered by the upper floor becomes yang, as shown in Figure 2.4. Therefore, position lofts over areas that will benefit from the yin quality. Good candidates are kitchens, bedrooms, bathrooms, studies, and children's playrooms. Figure 2.5 illustrates an entire floor plan using lofts to create yin and yang spaces in a vacation home.

If retrofitting existing space by adding a sleeping loft is not a structural option, consider sleep sofas, rollaway beds, Murphy beds that fold up into standing cabinets, or inflatable mattresses (the new ones, by the way, can be very comfortable).

Portable or permanent dividers easily remodel a space and, as suggested in Figure 2.6, can be permanent or temporary solutions. Suppose your computer is in the family room. A permanent or movable divider, low or high, can separate the computer space from the rest of the area. Dividers on tracks can carve out a temporary sleeping niche in a gathering space.

Figure 2.4 Even when there is not a great deal of "standing space" when on the loft, it can be an appropriate guest/child sleeping area. Instead of stairs, you can hook a ladder to the underside of the loft or install fold-down stairs to allow unencumbered movement below the loft.

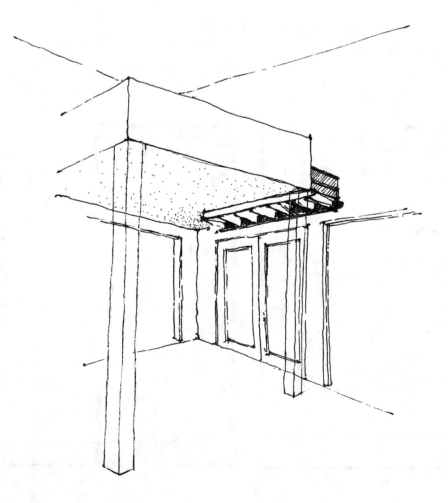

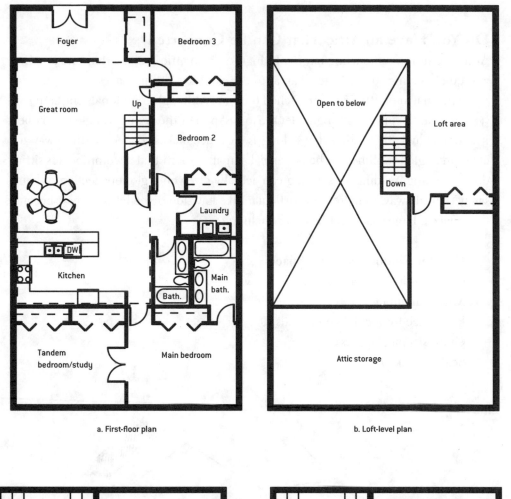

a. First-floor plan

b. Loft-level plan

Figure 2.5 With sufficient height between a floor deck (a) and a roof deck, it is possible to use a roof's cavity for a loft (b). The rooms under the loft will be more yin or cozy and those with the higher ceilings more expansive or yang.

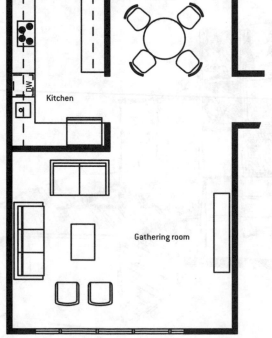

a. Before

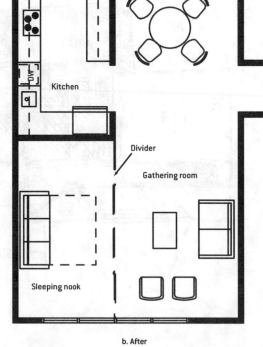

b. After

Figure 2.6 Dividers (b) can be permanent or temporary solutions to create flexible space.

Do You Have an Attic That Can Be Converted?

Attics are prime remodeling targets. In Figure 2.7 an attic is converted into an office and quiet reading space. Note all areas under eaves are sitting spaces.

The charm of attics is their pitched roofline. Although traditional feng shui cautions us that sleeping or sitting under the lowest part of the ceiling's angle fosters sickness or bad luck, the truth is that so long as the space makes you feel nestled away and cozy, an angled roofline can be beneficial. An attic room that accommodates sitting down working, reading, or sleeping can actually give you a glorious feeling of being safely tucked away. Children, in particular, like low sloping ceilings, in part because they make a large space feel less overwhelming.

Uses for Remodeled Attic Spaces

Cozy reading area and book repository

Music chamber

Play space for a child and friends

Guest sleeping spaces

Seated work areas

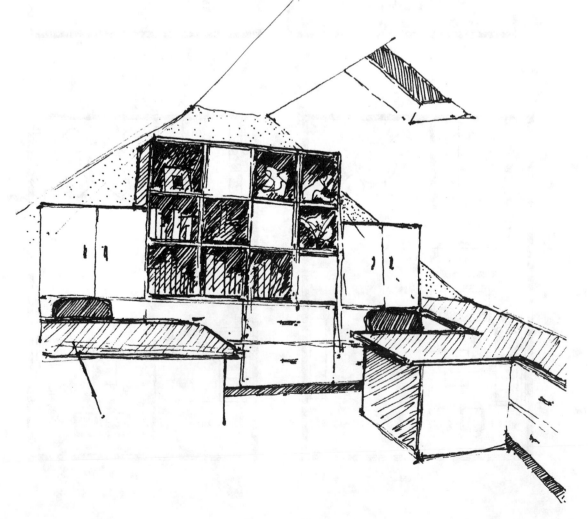

Figure 2.7 Attics don't have to be repositories for "stuff." Attic spaces are ideal for seated activities or activities not requiring a great amount of headroom.

Do You Have a Basement That Can Be Better Utilized?

All too frequently the basement turns into a home's permanent garbage pail. Situated below grade and not naturally lit, basements don't seduce us as other spaces do. If a basement will be used exclusively for nighttime activities, then the lack of natural lighting will not be an issue. What do you like to do in the evening that could benefit from privacy and isolation?

I grew up with a pool table in the basement. My dad, sister, and I would retire downstairs to "bond" while Mom cleaned up after dinner. (Today I wonder how we got away with not helping her.) After being slaughtered by Dad's cue stick, we would pop back upstairs to join Mom in the den. Are there special activities that your family likes? Would a yoga chamber, meditation spot, or hobby studio be used nightly? Figure 2.8 invites you to consider activities that would not be affected adversely by little or no natural light. Would a family member like to have a quiet space to study, experiment, or invent? Since a basement rarely has interior walls, how many activities can coexist?

Do You Have a Garage That Can Be Reconsidered?

Making a garage into an interior space is another option, especially in warm climates. The garage's replacement with a carport can be an architectural enhancement, as illus-

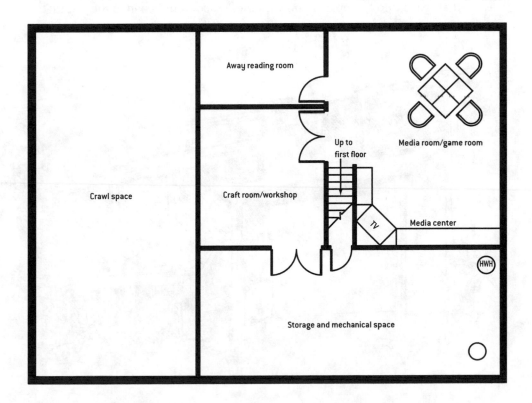

Figure 2.8 While an artificially lit area like a basement might not be attractive as a second gathering space, it could better be used for media entertainment areas, extra reading spaces, and hobby/craft areas.

trated in Figure 2.9, and is also a practical solution when there is not enough land for a conventional addition.

From a slide presentation by new urbanist Andres Duany, I observed how physical features contribute to human interactions and contentment. New urbanists understand that the building types and their relationships to each other shape the spirit of a neighborhood. In this presentation the garage was his prime example. A series of photographs followed the progression of the garage over time. They showed how the garage started as a small building set back behind a home, the kind where a small path with grass growing between dirt tracks led the family car to its enclosure. As time marched on, the garage moved forward too and now sat alongside the main house, though it was still detached from it. Later covered walkways would connect the house with the garage and protect the occupants from inclement weather as they walked from their car to the threshold. Finally, garages became directly connected to the house, and over the years garages edged forward. Today the "snout house" as we call it displays a garage consuming most of a home's front facade. In fact, the garage in a snout house devours more front footage than does the main entrance area. Feng shui's wisdom tells us that what is assigned the most space wields the most importance. Homes with "snouts" seem to tell us that cars have become more important than people! If you already live in a home where the garage is the predominant feature, converting that space into a people-friendly interior space would change the message of the facade and communicate the importance of its inhabitants over their vehicles.

Figure 2.9 The fanciful carport's projection adds character to the home's facade and permitted the garage's square footage to be converted into an interior living space in this home located in the southern United States.

Furthermore, there are health reasons why a garage should be separate from the living space. Toxins such as paints and cleaning agents typically end up in the garage, from where their vapors seep through the air ducts and doors into the home—not to mention the fumes spewed into the air each time a vehicle enters or leaves. An exterior shed or an insulated closet is a better storage space for these toxic solvents. Another solution is to add a foyer off the garage with a double door serving as a buffer between the garage and living space.

Have You Used the Hallways and Passage Spaces in Your Home?

Hallways and passage spaces can be more than walkways. Are you blessed with passageways that are both wide and high? In both cases, consider narrow built-ins to take care of storage needs, as shown in Figure 2.10. While we surrounded bedroom doors with narrow storage and shelves approximately six to eight inches wide, pantry storage in a hallway off a kitchen with a six-inch-wide shelf is all it takes to store cans, bottles, and packages of food that would otherwise be jammed into the kitchen cabinets after a trip to the supermarket.

Feng shui teaches us that order is a requisite for internal serenity and empowerment. With a place for everything mundane, finding the resolve to do what is necessary becomes easier.

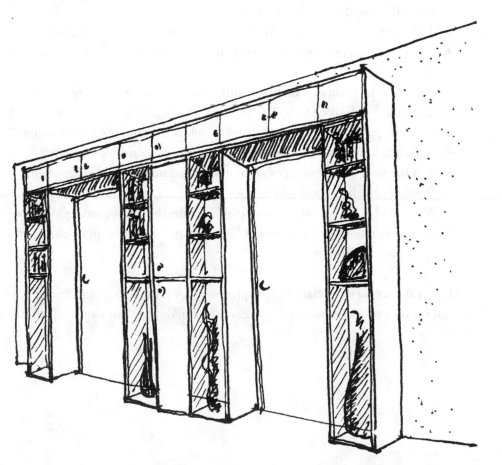

Figure 2.10 Storage units around doors increase the importance of the rooms they lead into while the extra storage/display offers convenience.

Can a Room Change Size to Breathe More Space into an Adjoining One?

Just as a dining room may be superfluous, the amount of space assigned to some rooms may be inappropriate. A living room used only occasionally because the family room fits most social purposes is an example of yet another space whose use is not commensurate with its size. A much-needed home office space could be carved out of a little-used living room. A desk unit with doors that shut would allow a living room to maintain its character for formal occasions. If you retrofit underused spaces to include the functions that you need, costly additions may be unnecessary.

When to Build an Addition

Sometimes remodeling won't fully satisfy your changing needs, or it may even create new problems while solving others. Answer the following questions about your remodeling plans to see if an addition might be a better idea after all.

After Remodeling . . .
- Will the main gathering areas still be too small for the number of people who will typically be using them?
- Will there be enough room for organized, accessible storage spaces?
- Will the rooms used most frequently have appropriate visual connections to the outdoors?
- Will there be sufficient kitchen, bathroom, and work area counter space?
- Is there enough space to update the most frequently used entrance, even if it's to the garage or kitchen, so that it is welcoming and not just utilitarian?
- Will each family member's individual interests have sufficient space?
- Will the plan incorporate design modifications necessitated by any family member's medical condition?
- Will the plan accommodate predictable future changes or enlarged households (when a new baby arrives, if "Boomerang" adult children return, or aging parents move in)?

If you answer no to several of these questions, the remodeling might not give you enough for your money, and you might consider building an addition that will serve these needs.

The connections between old spaces and new construction need to be carefully considered as well. In feng shui terms graceful connections and transitions relate to the Tao. The movement and flow should feel natural and purposeful, and there should be some references to old as well as new in both spaces. In architectural terms this translates into additions that respect the integrity of the existing house, taking into account its proportions, details, and consistency of materials. The addition must not inappropriately interrupt the flow throughout the entire space. Moreover, the Tao concept of "memory of place" (a smooth transition between what was and what has been changed) should be considered by carrying over elements from the old part of the house to the new addition. For example, if every room in your home has wall light switches forty-two inches from the floor, placing a new one fifty-four inches from the ground will disrupt the memory of place for that detail. Here are some ways to implement memory of place.

How to Infuse Memory of Place into an Addition
- Place light switches at the same height and the same side of the door as they are in the older part of home.
- Continue flooring from the original part through at least the entrance of the new space.
- Repeat the location of ceiling light fixtures, trim, or the use of color.
- Place at least some of the windows at the same height, size, or proportion as in the existing home.
- While it is practical to install the latest well-insulated, low-maintenance windows and doors in an addition, matching the old-style window or door helps fuse the new with the old.
- Other items to consider repeating are grilles, hardware, and millwork details.

When existing characteristics are ignored, the addition is nothing more than a box plopped onto the side of a house as a repository for space. Additions should be planned thoughtfully and function like a child who inherits the best from each parent while still being unique.

Whether your ultimate choice is remodeling, adding on, buying, or building, uncovering the answers to the questions posed in this chapter will lend clarity to your choice. If your requirements for a neighborhood can be satisfied elsewhere, you might want to buy or build rather than remodel. Whether it makes sense to buy depends on how you can make the space conform to your own needs. If you are ready to embrace the challenge of building, answering the questions in this chapter will provide a basis for creating spaces that will serve you well.

Changes in your physical environment can lead to personal growth. Although change might at first seem daunting and overwhelming, know that the freedom and relief provided by change starts as soon as the planning process begins. Without change, we stagnate. Make changes today in the best way you know how, but remember that you cannot live forever with what works for today. The only permanent thing in this world is change. Embrace its reality.

3

Lifestyle Meets Housing Style

Before buying, building, or remodeling, it's important to determine what style of home suits you best. While this chapter deals mainly with freestanding housing, the concepts can be applied to townhouses and one- or two-story condominiums and apartments. This chapter is mainly for those starting from scratch, but if your remodeling plans include the option of a major addition, you too might be able to benefit from the following material. Lifestyle and family composition should be the main determinants of housing style. Aesthetics are a powerful component, but it is more important that a space accommodate your specific habits and needs than that it be simply pleasing to the eye. The arrangement of rooms, the position and style of windows and doors, and the number of levels shape the behavior of a home's inhabitants. Here's our take on how to select a housing style for different family configurations and lifestyle factors.

Traditionally, floor plans include rooms designated as living rooms, dining rooms, and family rooms. We encourage you to rethink these names and the defined uses of these rooms and reinvent your gathering spaces to meet your own unique requirements. Take an average midlife couple in their late thirties or early forties with children between the ages of eight and fifteen. At this stage in life many couples are approaching their economic apex and want to go for the "big" or "last" house. The current trend says that bigger is better. But is that best for this family or for you? Instead of looking for a "mansion" with expansive, oversized living, dining, family, breakfast, sun, and exercise rooms, plus a separate home office, library, guest wing, etc., why not choose or create smaller flexible, multipurpose gathering spaces? Feng shui's wisdom suggests that when a structure is large or has more rooms than a family can comfortably use each day, it can be wasteful and negative. Many of us have experienced a hunger when dining out that we believed needed to be satisfied by large amounts of food. Often in such instances we leave a great deal uneaten, thus wasting food. In the same way, a home should provide the right amount of nourishment, not more than

"We shape our buildings and our buildings shape us."

WINSTON CHURCHILL

we can possibly absorb. A larger gathering room may be suitable for entertainment and should have built-in cabinets for media equipment; a second smaller one may have details like hardwood bookshelves and comfortable seating for family relaxation and a casual gathering of a small group of people. When we assign a nonentertainment use to a secondary gathering space, the house offers more options and avoids repetitive applications so that each room is used regularly. Toss aside developers' advertisements in the real estate section of your Sunday paper that list amenities considered mandatory for "graceful" living and really rethink what kinds of spaces will support your daily existence.

Also keep in mind as you review the plans in this chapter that they are not meant to be blueprints but rather to exemplify a general housing type. Use your imagination to extend the basic idea to the variations that would serve your family. Figure 3.1 depicts a three-bedroom ranch house, but a single-story house can have more or fewer bedrooms and still fall into the same category as long as the bedrooms are contiguous and not separated by gathering spaces.

Four Basic Housing Types

1. A traditional ranch, a one-story structure with all bedrooms on one side of communal rooms, as shown in Figure 3.1
2. A split ranch, a one-story structure with a master suite on one side of the communal rooms and the other bedrooms on the opposite side, as illustrated in Figure 3.2
3. A two-story structure with the communal rooms on the grade level and bedrooms on the second level, with potential use of attic and basement levels, as depicted in Figure 3.3
4. A split-level house with the main communal rooms on a middle level, the bedrooms on the upper level, and ancillary rooms on the lower level, as shown in Figure 3.4

Which Housing Style Is Best for Your Family Configuration?

Before you read on, take these self-tests to give you an indication of which style home might best suit your family configuration. All adult family members should answer these questions. Answer yes or no based on how you feel most of the time. You can determine how strong your preferences are for one-story or multistory living based on the number of affirmative answers you gave. You may have a strong preference for a two-story feature but find all of your other preferences more aligned to the single story.

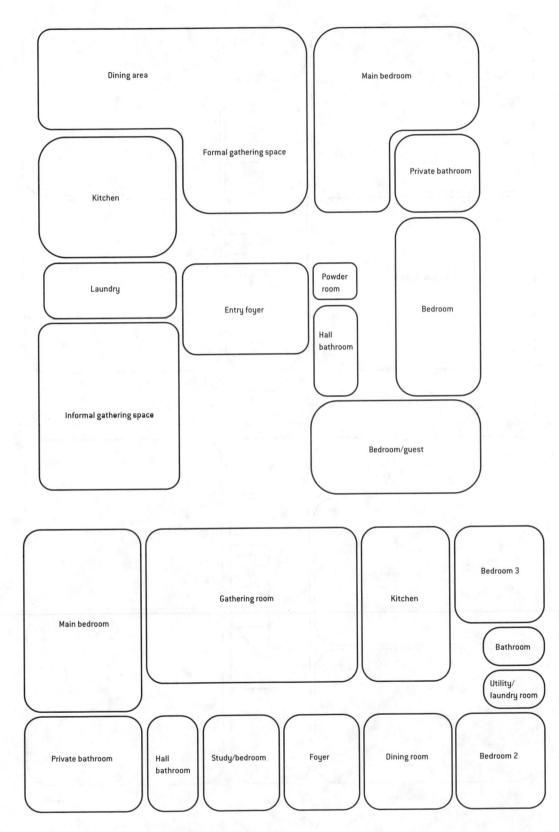

Dining area

Main bedroom

Formal gathering space

Private bathroom

Kitchen

Laundry

Entry foyer

Powder room

Hall bathroom

Bedroom

Informal gathering space

Bedroom/guest

Gathering room

Kitchen

Bedroom 3

Main bedroom

Bathroom

Utility/laundry room

Private bathroom

Hall bathroom

Study/bedroom

Foyer

Dining room

Bedroom 2

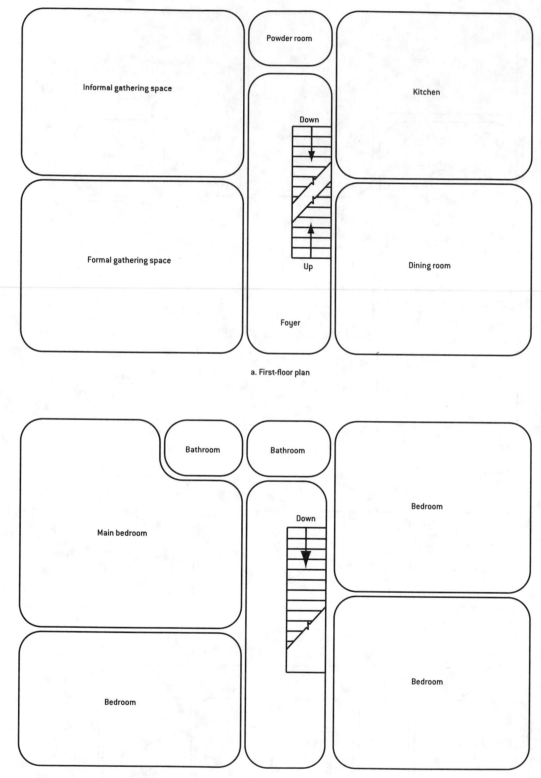

Figure 3.3 In a typical two-level structure the common rooms are usually on the lower level (a) and bedrooms are on the upper one (b). If a basement exists, it is often a repository for laundry, heating and cooling, storage, and flexible common space.

Informal gathering space

Powder room

Kitchen

Down

Formal gathering space

Up

Dining room

Foyer

a. First-floor plan

Bathroom

Bathroom

Bedroom

Main bedroom

Down

Bedroom

Bedroom

b. Second-floor plan

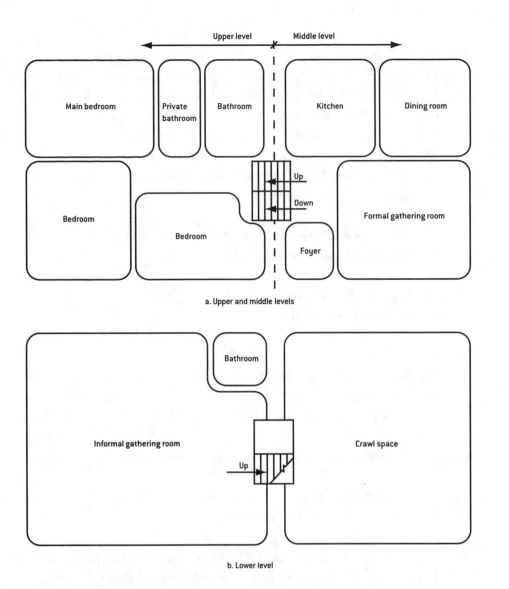

a. Upper and middle levels

b. Lower level

Figure 3.4 A split-level home typically has the kitchen/dining/formal gathering space on the mid level (a), the bedrooms on the upper (a), and the informal gathering space on the lower level (b).

For example, you may like your home office to be sequestered from all of the other rooms, but find that all of your other answers suit one-story living. In this case you need to consider finding a way to sequester the office through a level change, a hallway turn, or another inventive architectural feature that will fulfill this requirement without having to move into a two-level house. If you have a strong preference that supports an entirely different housing type from most of your other answers, be creative in supporting it by modifying the dominant housing type.

Which Housing Style Suits a Family with Children
1. I like to be within earshot or visual distance of my child.
2. It is important to me to have my child feel bold and unafraid of exploring.
3. I get uncomfortable when my children retreat to their private spaces.

4. I want my child to act independently and not require constant supervision.
5. I find that parents who spend only mealtimes with their children miss out on much of their experience.
6. If I am present, my child relies far too much on my input.
7. I want my home to reflect my children's interests and needs.
8. It is very important for me to have "grown-up" rooms without children's toys, games, or paraphernalia.

One-floor living probably suits your needs if you answered yes to 1, 3, 5, and 7. Multifloor living probably suits your needs if you answered yes to 2, 4, 6, and 8.

Which Housing Style Suits a Family with Only Adults Who Work Away from Home

1. After I return home, I like to have time by myself before I engage in conversation and partnership activities.
2. It is important to me to relate the events of my day as soon as possible to family members.
3. I like to check the answering machine or mail before changing clothes or starting dinner.
4. I prefer to relax and engage in conversation before I begin the evening activities.
5. There is nothing I like more than spending time outside in the garden or doing some exercise as soon as I get home.
6. I need a special place to meditate on arriving home at the day's end.
7. The sound of the radio or television disturbs me when I return home.
8. To me a house bustling with activity is central to feeling at home and loved.
9. When I get home, I prefer to relax with solitary pursuits before I start cooking the evening meal.
10. The sounds of family members' chatter in the background feel comforting to me.

One-floor living probably suits your needs if you answered yes to 2, 4, 5, 8, and 10. Multifloor living probably suits your needs if you answered yes to 1, 3, 6, 7, and 9.

Which Housing Style Suits a One-Person Household

1. I feel isolated and depressed when I don't have a variety of spaces to use.
2. I have, however slightly, a sense of fear or dread when there are places in my home that are not visually or easily accessible to me.

3. I love to use each of my living spaces for individualized activities and use a great deal of wall space to hang up objects of art.

4. I feel safer when my bedroom is relatively far away from the gathering spaces.

5. I feel more comfortable being within close reach of all the rooms in my home.

6. I would love to own an alarm system with a panic button near my bed.

7. Whether or not I have experienced this, it seems comforting to have a door that opens to the outside from almost every room.

8. I imagine living in the turret of a castle would feel like a very protected place.

9. I do not like my home office to be in visual contact with other spaces because I tend to be distracted by their lure.

One-floor living likely suits your needs if you answered yes to 2, 5, 6, and 7. Multifloor living likely suits your needs if you answered yes to 1, 3, 4, 8, and 9.

Which Housing Style Suits Those Combining Home with Workplace

1. I like to hear the sounds of family activities in my home while I'm working.

2. I often feel isolated from my family when working.

3. I hate distractions when I work.

4. I find listening to music comforting whether working or doing other activities at home.

5. Whenever I pass my workspace outside of my normal business hours, I start thinking about work again.

6. I work all the time.

7. I have to be coaxed away from other activities before I enter my workspace.

8. I hate it when my work materials are spread all over my home.

One-floor living probably suits your needs if you answered yes to 1, 2, 4, and 7. Multifloor living likely suits your needs if you answered yes to 3, 5, 6, and 8.

The Traditional Ranch Layout

The ranch-style house (shown in Figure 3.1) emerged during the post–World War II housing boom and basically consisted of the communal rooms—kitchen, living room, and dining room—on one side and the bedrooms on the other. The plumbing was often placed back to back and the original version had only one living room, but soon another gathering space was added to the popular ranch house. This room has been called the *finished basement, den, family room,* or today's *great room.* As time progressed, the original living room grew smaller while the second, more casual, living space grew larger.

In my childhood home the formal living room was far larger than the family's den. This second living space was nothing more than a porch converted to indoor space. Since the room was long and narrow, our family had to sit like ducks in a row on the two adjacent couches. There was not much we could do as a family except watch television and, since the living room was off-limits for children, my sister and I played separately in our bedrooms a great deal.

Today's ranch is far more likely to have a larger great room and a smaller formal gathering space. Before building or renovating, decide how to apportion the space for these two gathering spaces and consider whether it is even necessary to have both.

Assigning several uses to a space is a creative way to live. Would a screen placed between the kitchen and dining area in a great room change a casual atmosphere into a formal one? It is much less expensive to install a custom-made roll-down screen than it is to build a room! Could a preexisting formal dining room be freed up for other uses? Are you starting a business working out of your house? Could a formal living room be converted to a home office? These and other questions will be answered specifically in Chapter 6, but let these thoughts roll around in your mind as you learn more about how different house styles mesh with different lifestyles.

How Families with Children Are Affected by a Traditional Ranch Layout

Children and adults require both communal and private spaces. In Western households children usually have more opportunities for a private space of their own than they do in traditional households in the Far East. However, a ranch-style house without a basement or an attic doesn't always afford adults personal, private spaces except for a shared bedroom. While at least 50 percent of the home should be devoted to communal family activity, each family member ought to have some private space as well.

In many cases the best solution is shared personal space. Not all personal space needs to be in bedrooms. Carving out space to accommodate computers, hobby areas, and other individual activity centers outside of bedrooms is a practical way to allocate personal space without physically separating family members from one another. This solution can improve family communication while providing private space, but the layout of a ranch home clearly needs to be rethought to accommodate it. Try to imagine places for furniture besides those you feel "should" house certain pieces. Also plan windows, shelves, and lighting to accommodate shared personal spaces. Figure 3.5 shows how a fairly common layout can provide alternatives depending on a family's needs.

How Couples Without Children Are Affected by a Typical Ranch Layout

One-floor living affords a couple ease of contact. If you have ever felt frustrated looking for your partner, whether by voice or on foot, or resented being separated from the "action," then one-floor living is for you.

One-floor living may not necessarily suit fiercely independent individuals or those who cherish privacy or require quiet and tranquillity. Here's a short test to ascertain some of your requirements for personal space.

Personal Space Requirements
1. I find it hard to concentrate when I can hear conversation or the sound of television.
2. I concentrate best with background music.
3. The sound of footsteps past my room gives rise to apprehension that I am about to be disturbed.
4. Isolation makes me uncomfortable, and I concentrate best when the vibrations of life surround me.
5. I prefer to live in a city.
6. I prefer to live in the country.
7. I prefer daytime to nighttime hours.
8. I prefer nighttime to daytime hours.

Answering yes to questions 2, 4, 5, and 7 indicates a one-story house is better suited to your nature. Answering yes to questions 1, 3, 6, and 8 indicates a two-story house may be better suited to your nature. Of course you should not rely solely on the results of this simple test, and there are ways to answer your needs for personal space besides exchanging your one-story house for a multistory house or vice versa. For example, a person who shows a strong preference for one-story living but happens to live in a two-story house might create a private niche on the main gathering floor for hobbies or desk-related activities. Conversely, a person with a test revealing a preference for two-story living who resides in a one-level structure might create a soundproof space for personal activities as far away as possible from a home's gathering spaces.

Figure 3.5 (a)
Typical furniture
layout does not
provide for any
personalized spaces
for individual inter-
ests. (b) A play area
is created instead of
the more typical
dining area so a
young child can be
seen from both the
kitchen and the
gathering area.

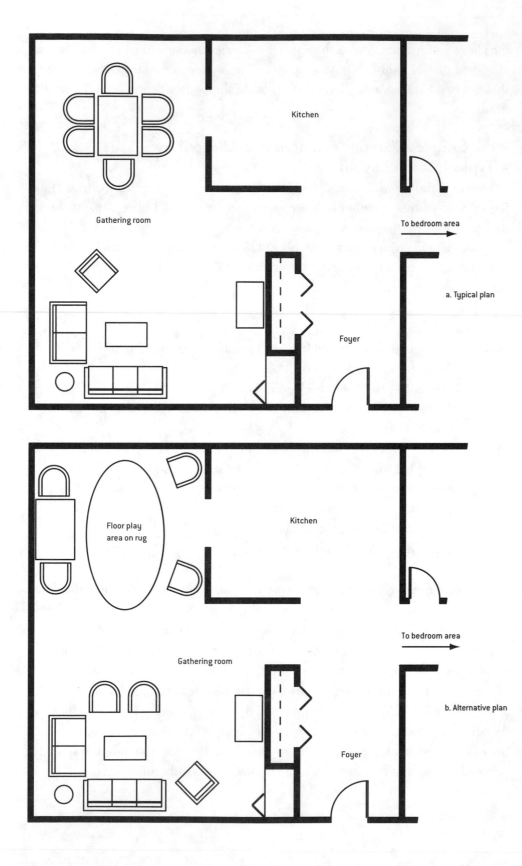

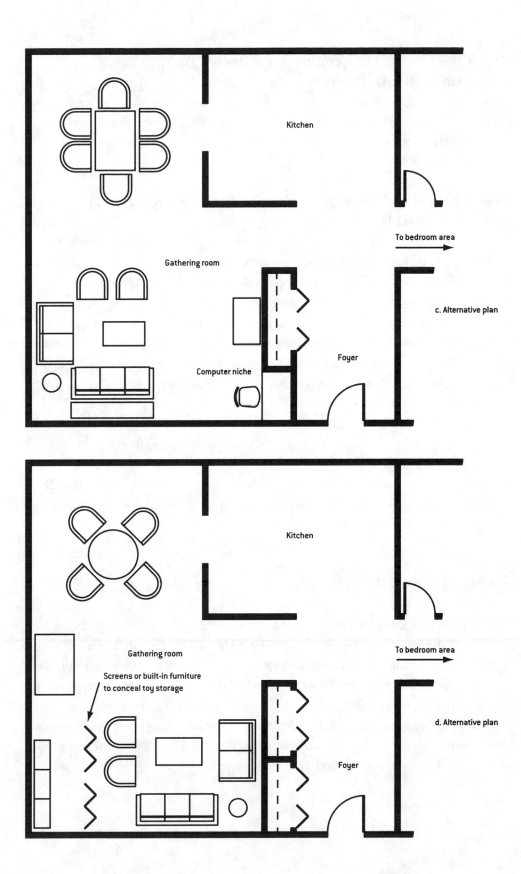

Kitchen

To bedroom area

Gathering room

Computer niche

Foyer

c. Alternative plan

Kitchen

To bedroom area

Gathering room

Screens or built-in furniture
to conceal toy storage

Foyer

d. Alternative plan

Figure 3.5 (c) Moving the seating units closer together in a gathering space allows a computer niche to be integrated into the main family room. (d) A freestanding or ceiling-mounted screen can block toys or workspace and/or hobby items from view in the main gathering space.

How One-Person Households Are Affected by a Traditional Ranch Layout

Unless you need to separate work from home or you have frequent out-of-town overnight visitors, as a single person you may very well benefit from one-floor living. However, should change be desirable, a two-story house or one with a more complex layout would be more suitable.

How Those Combining Workplace and Home Are Affected by a Traditional Ranch Layout

Having a workplace and your bedroom close together may encourage you to work excessively. If the first room that you pass at daybreak and the last before bedtime is your home office, its importance will outbalance all other home activities.

With such a layout, it becomes imperative to use decoration and embellishments to distance the workspace from the rest of the home. For example, an unadorned window can have mullions placed inside, or a door can be lined with cork to add weight and, literally, a thickened sense of privacy. Storage places including files, bookshelves, or closets against a contiguous wall with hallways or common spaces can enhance the sense of privacy and of being in a nest.

Figure 3.6 shows how a home was remodeled to assist a recent widow gain appropriate space for a new business enterprise. She had shoved her office behind a door in one of two guest bedrooms. The guest bedrooms were not used more than once a year for her visiting adult children. Although she was reluctant to claim the east-facing guest bedroom as her own (a mother's guilt) she finally did so, placing a sofa bed in the room. Her new business took off.

The Split Ranch Structure

The split ranch (see Figure 3.2) is a one-story structure with the master bedroom on one side of the common rooms and the other bedrooms on the other. This may be an ideal living arrangement for people living solo. The master bedroom and living area are conveniently adjacent to each other, while the other bedrooms, serving ancillary functions such as guest rooms and workspace, are set off so that you don't have the feeling of living too close to your workspace or unused rooms. This polarization of bedrooms makes a single home function as two homes. Thus the home can expand when needed and yet not feel too large when unused.

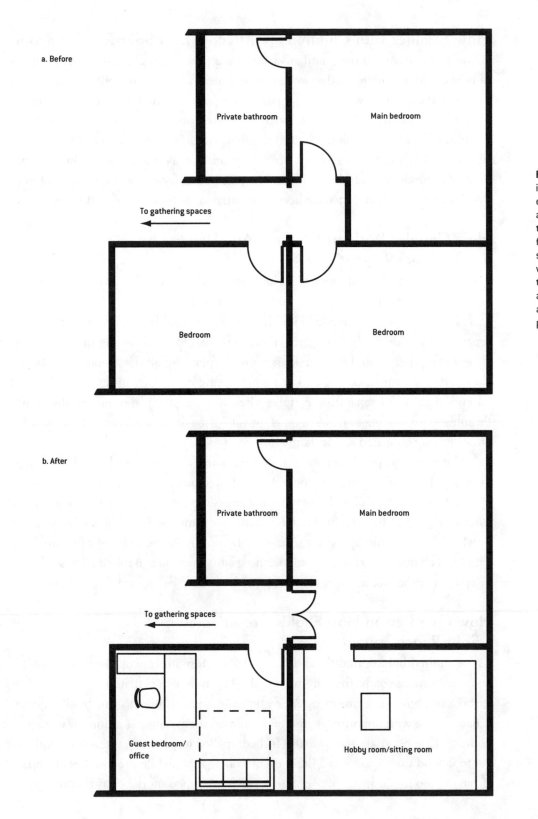

a. Before

Private bathroom

Main bedroom

To gathering spaces

Bedroom

Bedroom

b. After

Private bathroom

Main bedroom

To gathering spaces

Guest bedroom/office

Hobby room/sitting room

Figure 3.6 Changing the room's entrances and associative functions (a) allowed for a fuller use of space (b). The office was separated from the private rooms and subsequently acted as its own private wing.

How Families with Children are Affected by a Split Ranch Layout

A home that separates the guardians from those they guard challenges the intent of family. Children talking to themselves, crying silent tears before bedtime, or doing a lip-synch dance of joy are important parental experiences that distance may deny us. How can we be the emotional sentinels if we are not near our children? Distances seem much wider to a toddler than to an adult, and linear feet can, emotionally, feel like miles. Even baby monitors do not bridge this gap. Not that every split-bedroom floor plan produces disturbed children, but there is a danger of losing track of children's inner lives should their bedrooms be situated far from those of their parents.

How Couples Without Children Are Affected by a Split Ranch Layout

This configuration could prove ideal for couples without children who like to entertain frequently or need accessible and plentiful space to pursue hobbies or work. A spare bedroom can be converted into a library or a cozy game room. With extra rooms separated from the main living area, there's no need to put a sewing machine away, close a computer behind cabinet doors, or find a place for all the accoutrements that are unattractive and awkward and just don't belong in a gathering space. This is not an endorsement of separating couples when they engage in home activities but a thumbs-up for making available a quiet, private place or simply having the advantage of not feeling obligated to constantly tidy up.

This plan also provides ease of mobility should anyone be or become impaired by physical limitations. In 2002, some states enacted building requirements supported by the Americans with Disability Act—doorways wide enough to permit a walker or wheelchair to pass through, no-step front entrances, and showers that can be accessed by wheelchairs. Naturally, existing one-story homes are far easier to retrofit than those with level changes, and for those approaching late middle age, it might be wise to consider a home that could accommodate a suddenly disabled person.

How One-Person Households Are Affected by a Split Ranch Layout

As mentioned before, traditional feng shui texts admonish people not to inhabit a home with more rooms than are used daily. The rationale is that people who fail to partake of abundance are in essence allowing opportunities to slip by. Feng shui equates space with opportunity; therefore unused rooms suggest failure to seize possibilities. Like other animals, we also feel compelled to protect our territory, and trying to defend excess space is a drain on our energy. So, while the emotional impact of having too much space may not be as obviously uncomfortable as that of having too little, we need to be aware that unused spaces do have a negative impact on our personal and economic resources.

Many people end up living alone following the departure of grown children, the death of a spouse, or a divorce. Although decisions about giving up the family home are fraught with emotion at these times, it's important to understand that remaining alone in a home with unused rooms or spaces creates subconscious stress. One choice for those who prefer to stay where they are is to find ways to use every space or break down walls to enlarge the rooms that are used and eliminate those that aren't. If a move from a much beloved neighborhood would be too stressful, a change in the home's configuration would make sense.

It may not be necessary to invest in structural changes to make an extra bedroom serve other needs. It's a matter of setting it up to serve those needs. Closets with pull-out drawers, new shelves, and other fitting arrangements can easily be made to house hobby materials. Always try to make use of all the square footage of a home as part of your daily routine.

Perhaps the greatest challenge for a single person living with the main bedroom on one side and the other across the central gathering area is to use the other bedrooms in ways that satisfy and augment personal growth and comfort. Making a connection should be your guiding image. The real downside of such a configuration is that one side can potentially be underused because it is outside the main traffic pattern.

How Those Combining Workplace and Home Are Affected by a Split Ranch Layout

For those who combine work and daily living within the confines of their home and do not have young children, the split ranch may be the best configuration of space. When the ancillary bedrooms are used for offices, the heart of the home becomes the fulcrum that balances work and play. However, it is important to consider the view you will have when exiting the room housing your office. If you have to go through the main gathering area on your way from office to kitchen or bathroom, you may feel distracted from working or, worse, irritated at the intrusion of work obligations on home life. The key is to consider what messages best support the two different experiences of work and relaxation.

Notice in Figure 3.7 the view when exiting the home office is appropriately the kitchen and bathroom rather than the socializing areas. Since this client's teenager was at school during the day, she could close the bedroom door and shut off that view. When working at home, it is not a good idea to position the office near reminders of other obligations or nonwork experiences.

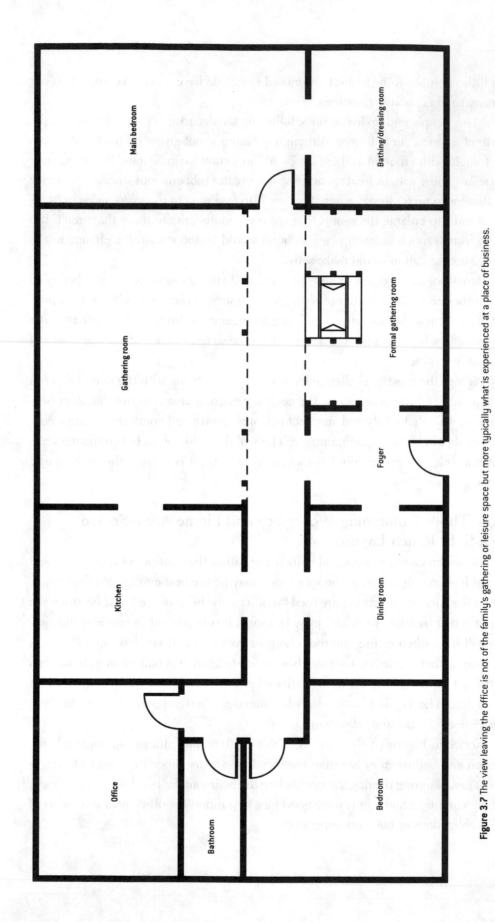

Figure 3.7 The view leaving the office is not of the family's gathering or leisure space but more typically what is experienced at a place of business.

The Two-Story Structure

The two-story home (see Figure 3.3) is the standard layout in many areas. Building upward rather than outward probably became common when families established businesses at the ground level and wanted their private quarters away from the work flow. In Asia and the Middle East, these "shop houses" date back hundreds of years. In colder climates two-story structures were also more efficient to heat than those sprawling out over one level. Attics and cellars evolved gradually, out of the necessity for food storage and to vent hot air or simply accommodate the unusable space created by steep rooflines.

How Families with Children Are Affected by a Two-Story Structure

The traffic pattern of the typical two-story dwelling seldom presents any confusion. With few corners to peer around, far-flung rooms, or split sleeping or gathering spaces, little effort is needed to uncover the whereabouts of other family members. Basically, the two main areas are private spaces and community spaces. For families with children, this is a far more satisfying scenario than the more complex one-story floor plans.

My friends Kate and Paul just bought a house matching this profile (see Figure 3.8) but with a slight twist. Instead of having all the bedrooms on the second floor, the house had two bedrooms upstairs and the master bedroom at the base of the stairs leading up to the children's sleeping rooms. Because of this layout, Kate and Paul's bedroom is fortunately positioned in a guardian location. I visited them the day after they moved in and asked what happened that first morning when their three- and five-year-olds woke up. They reported that the children simply scampered down the stairs into their bedroom to announce the start of the day. If the master bedroom is positioned off a pathway leading to and from the other bedrooms, it need not be adjacent to the children's bedrooms.

How Couples Without Children Are Affected by a Two-Story Structure

For a childless couple with a home office, a two-story structure may interfere with emotional closeness. If spouses tend to spend their leisure time on two different floors, this layout may reduce communication and connection. Unused extra bedrooms alongside a master bedroom stand as a symbol of emptiness. Don't confuse emptiness with sparseness, for the latter is a choice and the former is a result. Figure 3.9 shows how retractable walls can make an adjoining bedroom a flexible space without eliminating the option to close it off.

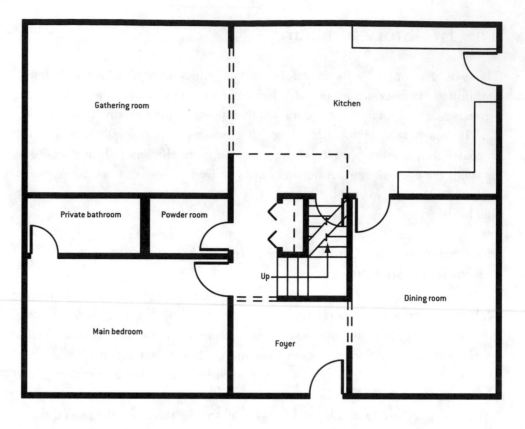

a.

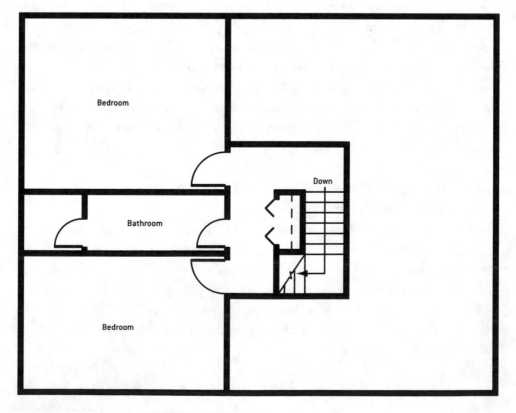

b.

Figure 3.8 Even though the main bedroom is downstairs (a), its location next to the stairway leading to the children's bedrooms (b) ensures it is still in the guardian position.

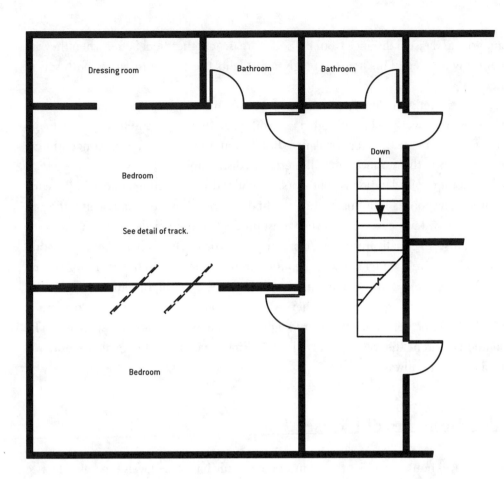

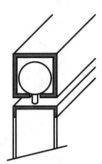

Figure 3.9 Creating a retractable wall can allow an unused space to become an additional adjacent one without compromising the occasional separateness required or creating a space too large for most of its requirements.

How One-Person Households Are Affected by a Two-Story Structure

So long as all the rooms serve specific functions on a regular basis, living in a two-story home affords a single person many choices and options. There is a catch, though, for singles with few indoor interests and hobbies. In the same way cabin fever develops in shut-ins, many spaces without diversity may contribute to boredom, loneliness, or depression.

On the other hand, some people feel uncomfortable without a sensorial awareness of their entire territory. In the same way children love small spaces, where their outstretched arms can touch the sides, some adults find that the ability to feel the perimeter of a home evokes security.

How Those Combining Workplace and Home Are Affected by a Two-Story Structure

It is appropriate for people who work at home, with or without children, to separate work from family life. This can be accomplished when the workspace is situated with auditory and visual distance from the social areas. Yet others feel better when they are centrally located. This house type gives residents the choice to satisfy both sets of needs.

The secret is to identify whether you are proximity or distance prone. If you scuttle away from work to be with others, a workspace that offers auditory or visual connection will create the proper balance. But if sounds prevent you from concentrating on your work, that connection will merely be distracting.

Another consideration is your work schedule. If you function at peak in the early morning, a spouse's morning routine might drive you crazy. In that case an office on the bedroom level can cut into your most productive time of day. Move your office downstairs. An equally frustrating, disrupting scenario exists when a person who works most productively at night locates the office on the same level as the gathering spaces.

Many couples have overlapping sleep schedules. One might remain in bed until eight in the morning, while the other rises at five. The same scenario could occur at night when one person reads past midnight while the partner falls asleep by ten. The solution could be the rotating walls shown in Figure 3.9 or a bedroom alcove buffered by a closet or hallway.

The Split-Level House

A split-level house (see Figure 3.4) most commonly has three levels separated by two staircases. With longer working hours and a larger variety of leisure activities, most of us need to carefully integrate convenience into a home. The location of the favorite gathering room on a different level from the kitchen is quite possibly the worst feature of the typical split-level plan. Converting the lower-level gathering space from a casual room to a formal one and using the "traditional" living room as the family room will allow family members to spend their precious family time together. However, in all plans where a kitchen and gathering space are contiguous, you may consider an alternative counter style like the split counter shown in Figure 3.10. Splitting a counter discourages what we believe is an inappropriate way for a family to dine together: having all family members seated along a counter, facing a space rather than each other. However, socializing with the cook during meal preparation is positive; with only two stools next to a counter, it is also more likely for those seated there to turn to each other as well as converse with the cook.

Three-level living may splinter family cohesiveness; therefore, delegating more shared family activities to the midlevel rather than the lower level can mitigate fragmentation.

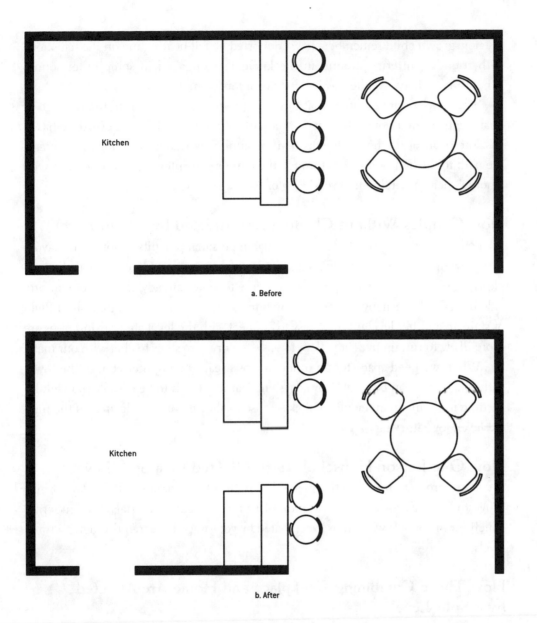

a. Before

b. After

Figure 3.10 Split a high kitchen counter so that it is not used exclusively as a family dining surface and so that the cook does not become a short-order chef.

How Families with Children Are Affected by a Split Level

A split-level layout may benefit a traditional family unit as long as the family's casual gathering space is on the same level as the kitchen. The lower space can include a private area, computer center, hobby area, or library.

For families with young children bedrooms up a short flight of stairs can support the desirable connection between gathering spaces and children's bedrooms. It is definitely beneficial to be a short bound up the stairs from a child who needs help. Also, my now-grown child remembers how comforted he felt hearing me on the telephone with friends, puttering around in the kitchen or engaged in some other sound-generating activity after he was bedded down for the night.

The other positive feature that this style promotes is frequent traffic through or near the heart of a home. To reach other parts of a split-level house, everyone has to pass the heart of the home. Even when the family's entrance is through the garage, the path to the bedrooms leads through the home's epicenter. Close connection with a home's heart is vital to the well-being of family members.

How Couples Without Children Are Affected by a Split Level

If a couple needs no private space to engage in personal pursuits at home, this layout can prevent unity because it provides two gathering options. Conversely, if the couple is retired and otherwise spends much time together already, this layout will provide beneficial alternative spaces in which to spend time alone. Again, a short flight of stairs to another level makes it easy to connect with the level above. Most of us are more likely to run up five stairs than to scale ten or more steps to chat with our mate.

When we need space for an office, hobby area, or computer center, the lower gathering space can be ideal. Nowadays entertaining tends to be casual, and with little time for home maintenance it makes sense to allocate one single area, at the middle level, for gathering.

How One-Person Households Are Affected by a Split Level

If you are prone to misplace things and generally a bit disorganized, this layout may prove to be disastrous. The frustration of trying to locate materials, remembering which room you left what in, is exacerbated by your need to search through all three levels.

How Those Combining Workplace and Home Are Affected by a Split Level

A three-level home satisfies the spatial requirements of a home office admirably. The lower level would serve best as the office space even if clients don't visit. Should clients often visit the office, build a door cordoning off this space. A door to the outside that bypasses the central living area affords an office a more orthodox feel, as shown in Figure 3.11. If the lower level is used for an office, a sliding screen in front of the stairs is another way to eliminate visual access to a home's private space.

Further, if an upstairs hallway is visible from the gathering space, consider decorating it in a way that is more visually appropriate to the lower level. Bookshelves, niches for sculpture, or light-drenched walls of paintings encircled with molding will

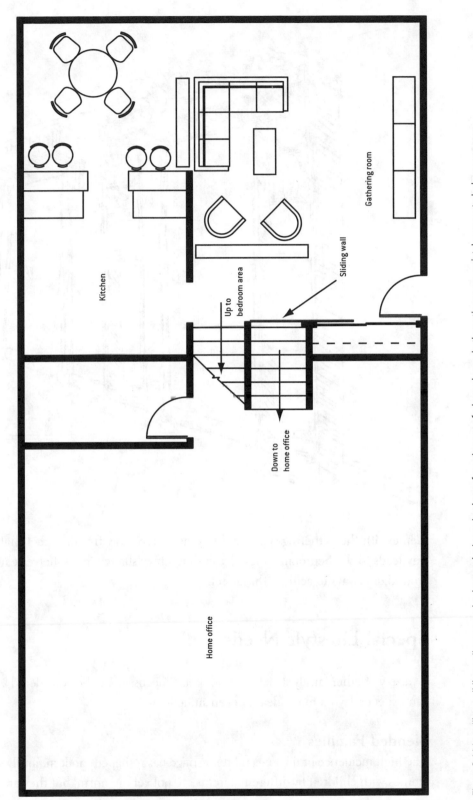

Kitchen

Gathering room

Sliding wall

Up to
bedroom area

Down to
home office

Home office

Figure 3.11 Installing a sliding wall to conceal a downstairs home business from the rest of a home keeps both sections appropriately separated when necessary.

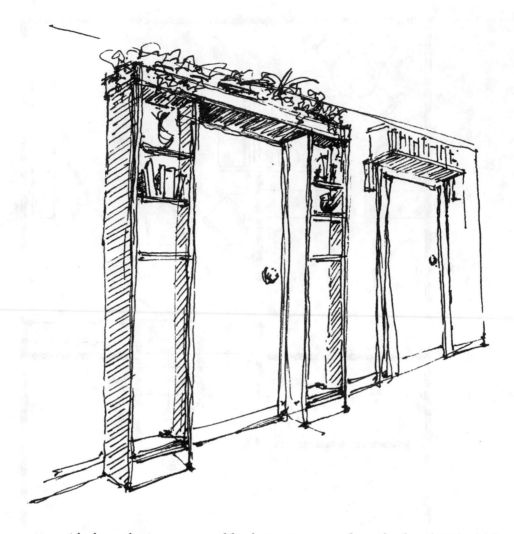

Figure 3.12
Surrounding a bedroom door with shelves can add to a sense of privacy of personal space or convert a feature-less hall into a visually inter-esting space.

merge with the gathering space and lead attention away from the fact that the hall-way leads to the bedrooms. Figure 3.12 shows how shallow bookshelves can be built around doorways to achieve this affect.

Special Lifestyle Needs

A variety of other family structures and special needs should be considered before you can expect a layout to be ideal or even suitable.

Blended Families

The high incidence of divorce and remarriage has reshaped modern family structure. Homes with children by different parents are not yet the norm, but they are certainly not a rare phenomenon, and more often than not the strain of blending children from different families creates stresses far above the inevitable stresses in traditional households.

The most problematic mix might be if one parent brings an only child into a new marriage where there are already two or more children. The only child may be at a disadvantage in the sense that he or she does not come to the new family with sibling support. Feng shui embraces the notion of righting inequities by balancing them in a physical space. Figure 3.13 suggests seating the outsider child in a blended family to the right of the parent or sibling with whom it is necessary to connect emotionally, especially while dining. Consider the following ways to right an uneven distribution of power by assigning the only child one or more of the following:

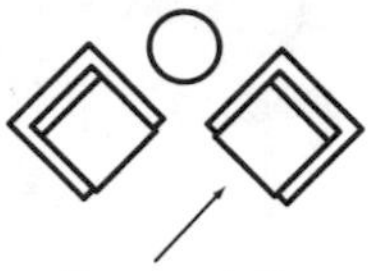

- A bedroom closest to the parents
- The biggest bedroom or one with a special feature
- A command position at the dining room table
- A dining room seating position to the right of the child's natural parent
- Colors other than dark blues for the bedroom
- Patterns with stripes in the bedroom
- The color adobe or salmon as an accessory color in the bedroom

Other considerations to assist family blending:

- Choose a round dining room table.
- Avoid a solitary chair position in a gathering space; always provide group seating.
- Be sure to have equally comfortable seating for all members.
- Locate the guardians' bedroom near the children's, especially when they are young.

Families Living with Aging Parents or Returning Children

Integrating aging adults into a preexisting family structure is often fraught with problems. When you build, renovate, or remodel, you should include the physical accommodations recommended by the Americans with Disabilities Act, as illustrated in Figure 3.14. These include but are not limited to wheelchair accessibility to the home and bathroom, and supports like railings to make physical movement safe and less daunting for an aging parent.

Hearing impairments are a common consequence of advanced years. This means that a television, radio, or stereo may end up tuned to decibels irritating to other fam-

Figure 3.13 Conversation is received emotionally rather than intellectually when addressed to a person's right ear.

Person seated here will receive messages more emotionally than intellectually

Figure 3.14 This chart shows accessability considerations for bathrooms.

With a bit of foresight and minimal expense, bathrooms can be planned to adapt to a variety of situations as needed at a later date, such as wheelchairs or walkers. A few ideas are:

1. Removable cabinets that can be replaced later with an open-front sink for accommodating a wheelchair
2. Adjustable counters
3. An accessible shower
4. Reinforced walls. Walls can be reinforced with 3/4" plywood or with wood blocking installed between the studs. This inexpensive reinforcement will provide for installation of any future grab bars, sink towel bars, and shower seat.
5. All plumbing controls should be lever type for easy operation.

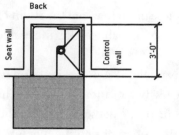

If space is at a premium, smaller showers are an option, with the inclusion of a shower seat. However, this layout will not accept a wheelchair, and attention must be paid to the location of grab bars, shower controls, and accessories to be within reach.

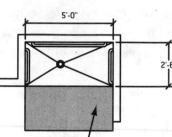

Recommended additional waterproof floor area for water control

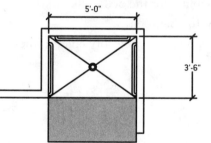

Shower Considerations:

1. Slip-resistant floors
2. Rounded corners
3. Curtains, not doors. Having neither is more easily accessible.
4. Handheld shower fixtures are best for wheelchair use and can also be clipped to the wall for use as a conventional shower.
5. Consider temperature controls:
   a. thermostatic control valves
   b. integral thermometer allowing temperature to be preset

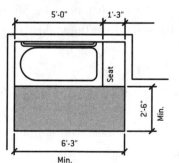

Bathtub Considerations:

1. Bathtubs can be difficult to get in and out of, particularly from a wheelchair. Sunken tubs for an elderly person can be practically impossible to negotiate. Therefore, the height of the tub should match the height of a wheelchair seat (approx. 19") or at least a comfortable chair height.
2. An extended tub deck (15" minimum), or a seat at the end of a bathtub is most helpful for transferring from a wheelchair.
3. A handheld shower used from the seat can be used for people who cannot lower themselves into a tub. Place the controls for easy seated access.
4. The bottom of the floor should be slip-resistant.

ily members. Providing them with a separate unit in their living space may be the answer but does not completely alleviate the problem until proper soundproofing can be installed.

If segregating an aging family member who is hard of hearing is not a positive option, get earphones for television or radio or place his or her chair closer to the source of sound. Also eliminate other household sounds around conversation areas, for the noises from appliance motors and the outside can interfere with communication. Figure 3.15 is a chart of standard soundproofing measures.

Visual acuity also diminishes with age. It can be difficult for older people to distinguish individual items in a drawer or closet unless bright lighting is installed. It may be a good idea to mount direct lighting over all drawers and closets if there are aging family members in a household. Lights that go on automatically when closet doors are opened is one more way of helping the family member function well in spite of reduced visual sharpness. In fact there is hardware that acts as a switch for closet lighting. When a door is opened, the light switches on, and then it turns off when the door is closed. This prevents frustration when trying to discern the contents of a closet. Also, painting or lining shelves and drawers with white or bright yellow makes object recognition easier.

The suggestions in this chapter are meant as a starting point for evaluating what living space will best serve you. You may find that some of the ideas trigger an awareness of feelings you have never articulated before. Remember, you build new, add on, or remodel to create a more fully connected experience with what you need and where you live. Your home is a like a second skin. As we shape our home, we shape our lives.

Sound Control

Unwanted sound (noise) can be controlled by absorbing the sound waves that create it. Soft materials (yin) absorb sound energy, while hard materials (yang) reflect it back into a space.

To create a quieter interior space, use more absorbent materials. Although absorbent materials could be used anywhere, ceiling treatments work better in large rooms, and wall treatments are more effective in smaller rooms.

Ceiling Treatments

Acoustical ceiling baffles: a series of vertical panels suspended from ceiling
    (larger areas, music rooms, gyms)
Banners: fabric draped along ceiling (various interior spaces)
Ceiling tile: acoustical tiles placed within a lay-in grid system (office areas, play
    areas—good for cross-talk reduction or masking mechanical noise)
Suspended ceiling panels: smooth panels suspended below another ceiling.

Wall Treatments

Acoustical wall panels: mounted on top of wall surface with clips, adhesive, Velcro,
    or magnetic tape (music rooms, studios)
Independent wall panels: freestanding from wall, room/space dividers. Anywhere
    privacy is required, prevents conversations from being heard in adjacent rooms
Wall tiles: adheres to wall surface (studio or media rooms)

General Rules (the denser or thicker the material, the more absorption)

Condition	Improvement
Light frame walls (wood or metal studs with drywall)	Add sound batt insulation Stagger studs
Single-layer drywall	Double-layer drywall
Wood flooring	Add rugs
Rock garden or wood fence	Add coniferous plants
Heavy walls (masonry, stone)	Fill cores with sand
Plaster	Furred-out surface
Carpeted flooring	Add padding
Thick shrubs	Add berm

The Parts That Make
the Whole

4

If you have ever looked at the boxes, squiggles, and hieroglyphics on a blueprint and wondered what in the world they mean, this chapter will enlighten you. Start with Figure 4.1, which will help you understand what the symbols on architectural plans mean. You can refer to this as needed throughout your building or remodeling projects. If you are already capable of reading a floor plan but have difficulty envisioning how the space will feel, this chapter will give you the tools to mentally transform a two-dimensional picture into a three-dimensional experience.

View a floor plan as if you are flying over a house without a roof and can see what is called the home's *footprint*, as shown in Figure 4.2.

Looking at a floor plan does not allow you to experience it in the same way you would if you stood at the threshold of each room. So when you study a floor plan, find the entrance of each room and imagine actually standing there. The next step is to visually think of raising the walls around you, as illustrated in Figure 4.3.

The ability to visualize a space in combination with an understanding of the floor plan, plus visiting the site to experience the relationship of the structure to its surroundings, will give you a feel for the finished home. Resizing and rearranging window heights, door swings, and lighting is far easier and cheaper to do in the planning stage.

"God is in the details."

LUDWIG MIES
VAN DER ROHE

Square Footage

Too often we misjudge what we see on paper and assume that a space designated for a specific purpose within a room is the right size and shape. To get a sense of the actual size of a space, use footsteps to measure out the dimensions listed on a floor plan, as in Figure 4.4. Assume that each step you take is the equivalent of about a foot when

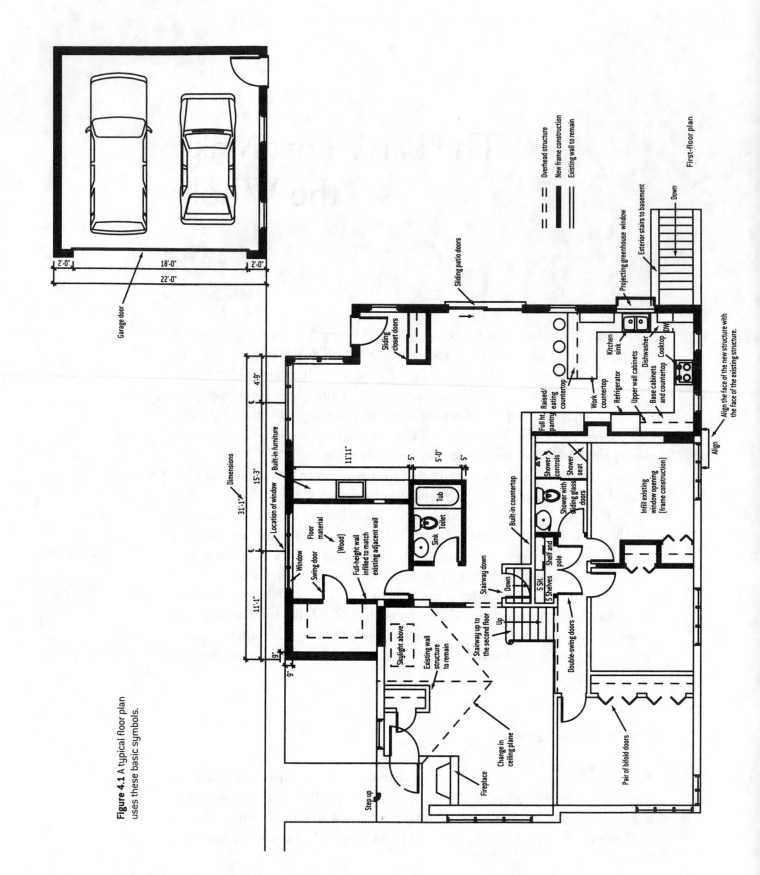

Figure 4.1 A typical floor plan uses these basic symbols.

First-floor plan

Down

Exterior stairs to basement

Projecting greenhouse window

Align the face of the new structure with the face of the existing structure.

Align

Infill existing window opening (frame construction)

Cooktop

DW

Base cabinets and countertop

Dishwasher

Upper wall cabinets

Kitchen sink

Refrigerator

Work countertop

Raised/ eating countertop

Full ht. pantry

Shower controls

Shower seat

Shower with sliding glass doors

Shelf and pole

5 Sh.
5 Shelves

Built-in countertop

Down

Double-swing doors

Pair of bifold doors

Sliding patio doors

Sliding closet doors

11'11"

5'
5'-0"
5'

Tub

Sink
Toilet

Stairway down

Stairway up to the second floor

Up

Change in ceiling plane

Fireplace

Step up

Existing wall structure to remain

Skylight above

Window

Swing door

Floor material

(Wood)

Full-height wall infilled to match existing adjacent wall

Built-in furniture

Location of window

Dimensions

31'-1"

15'-3"

11'-1"

9"

9"

4'-9"

Overhead structure

New frame construction

Existing wall to remain

Garage door

2'-0"
18'-0"
2'-0"

22'-0"

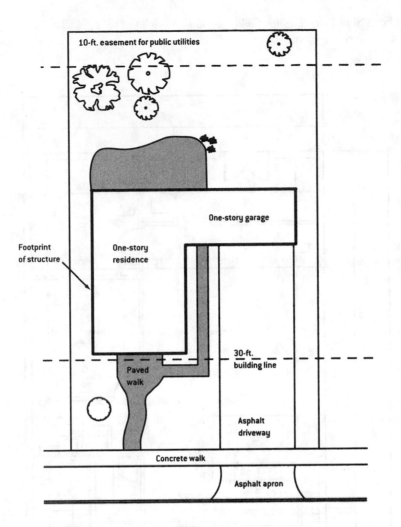
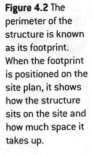

10-ft. easement for public utilities

One-story garage

One-story residence

Footprint of structure

30-ft. building line

Paved walk

Asphalt driveway

Concrete walk

Asphalt apron

Figure 4.2 The perimeter of the structure is known as its footprint. When the footprint is positioned on the site plan, it shows how the structure sits on the site and how much space it takes up.

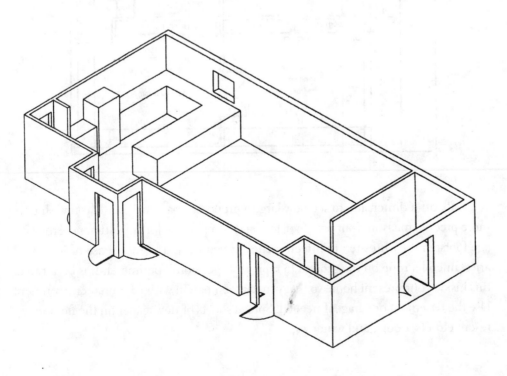

Figure 4.3 Visualizing the walls around you often feels very different from reviewing a two-dimensional floor plan. Use our technique to ascertain how the actual space will feel. Although we have recommended methods for determining a sense of horizontal size in reading floor plans, how a space will actually feel enclosed by the surrounding vertical structure is perceived quite differently. Features such as fenestration sizes and shapes, ceiling height, interior material and detail, lighting, color, and even outside views all impact the way an enclosed space is experienced.

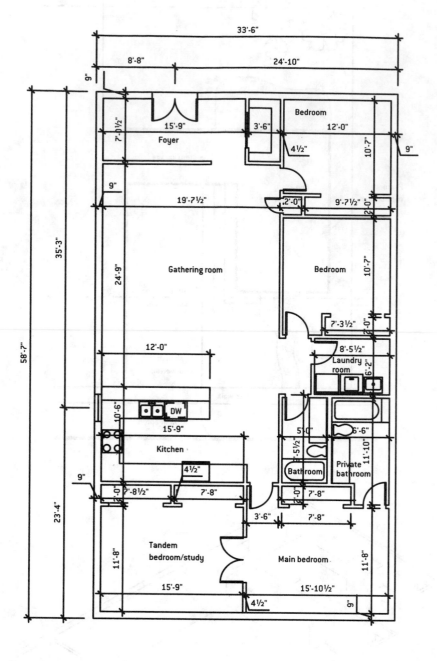

you walk off a dimension to see how large a proposed space will be. If you wish to be more precise, measure your own footsteps and compensate for any difference; the average footstep measures ten to fifteen inches. If you need a keener sense of its boundaries, uncoil a rope on the ground to represent the room's perimeter. It is better to do this inside your present home so that you can compare it with a familiar environment. Use the basement or garage if needed. Spread sheets of newspaper on the floor to represent closets, doors, and windows.

The Shape of a Room as Seen from the Threshold

The physical shape of a room can determine how you feel upon entering. Here are tips for determining whether the shape of a room is desirable when you are reading a floor plan.

Tips for Planning the Shape of Rooms

- It is more comfortable to walk straight ahead or turn right when entering a space, as you would in Figure 4.5a.
- A room with its longest side directly ahead, as illustrated in Figure 4.5b, is more likely to inspire use.
- A room that fans out horizontally from the entrance, as shown in Figure 4.5c, is less likely to inspire use than other shapes.
- If part of a room is concealed from the threshold, as shown in Figure 4.5d, those entering will feel on guard.
- A room with equal spaces in front and on both sides, like the one in Figure 4.5e, feels most stable.

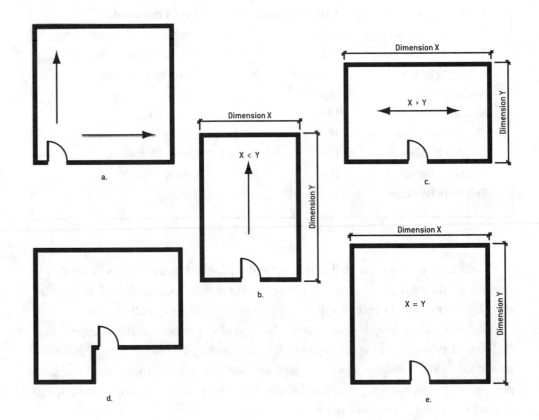

Figure 4.5 (a) It is more comfortable to walk straight ahead or turn right when entering a space. (b) A room with its longest side directly ahead is more likely to inspire use. (c) A room that fans out horizontally from the entrance feels less conducive to use than other shapes. (d) If part of a room is concealed from the threshold as shown, those entering will feel on guard. (e) A room with equal spaces in front and on both sides feels most stable.

Ceilings

Ceiling height may not be as relevant as floor space when you are trying to determine whether your furniture will fit into a room, but it does have a significant effect on how comfortable you will feel in the room. Ceiling heights that provide sufficient open space overhead will prevent you from feeling cramped, but ceilings that are too high will make you feel dwarfed. The proportion of height to square footage must be balanced delicately in spaces used daily. Ballroom-sized rooms with high ceilings won't work for most families' gathering rooms. They tend to feel intimidating and thus make people cluster in one small area, which is a waste of space. The following chart lists the feelings typically engendered by different ceiling heights in different rooms.

Remember, however, that "height" is a relative term based on where you live. For example, a modestly priced home in New Orleans might have a ten-foot high ceiling as standard, whereas in Pennsylvania the standard might be eight feet high.

SENSES IMPARTED BY DIFFERENT CEILING HEIGHTS IN DIFFERENT ROOMS

Room	Relative Height	Sense Imparted
Entrance	High	Impressed or overwhelmed
Entrance	Low	Pressured, compressed
Gathering Space	Adequate to high	Flexible; having options
Kitchen	High	Inspired
Kitchen	Low	Nurturing
Couple's Bedroom	High	Less intimate
Couple's Bedroom	Low	Close
Children's Bedroom	High	Lonely
Children's Bedroom	Low	Security

Generally, ceilings can be flat, tray, cathedral, vaulted, or arched, as illustrated in Figures 4.6 through 4.9. In feng shui, shape evokes certain feelings. The following list reveals the emotional overtones that various ceiling shapes will add to a room.

Varying ceiling heights or details can be a good way to alter a space's experience. If different types of ceilings are not viable, you can vary texture, lighting, and color or add skylights, moldings, coves, coffers, and rods for draping materials. For example, painting a high ceiling a dark color can make it feel lower; adding a skylight can give a low ceiling a sense of expansiveness.

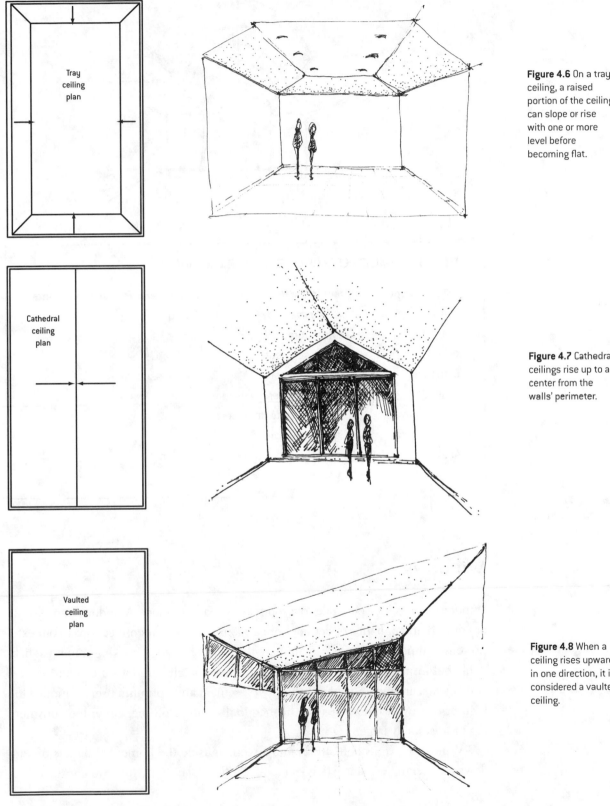

Figure 4.6 On a tray ceiling, a raised portion of the ceiling can slope or rise with one or more level before becoming flat.

Figure 4.7 Cathedral ceilings rise up to a center from the walls' perimeter.

Figure 4.8 When a ceiling rises upward in one direction, it is considered a vaulted ceiling.

Tray ceiling plan

Cathedral ceiling plan

Vaulted ceiling plan

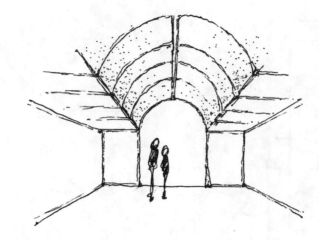

Figure 4.9 An arched ceiling curves upward either from the walls or from an edge of a flat ceiling.

THE EMOTIONAL EFFECTS OF DIFFERENT CEILING SHAPES

Ceiling Shape	Effect in the Room	Emotional Effect on Inhabitants
Flat	Nonintrusive	Safety
Tray	Creates intimacy under lower segments	Refuge
Cathedral	Magnet to center	Effortlessness
Vaulted	Divides the experience of a room into distinctly yin or yang areas	Attentiveness
Arched	Softens the defined volume	Freedom

Windows

Windows are as indispensable to a room as eyes are to a face. Windows can distract or comfort and enhance or detract from a room's use. As our connections to our exterior environment, windows can animate the spirit of a space, making it not just habitable but inspirational. However, placed inappropriately, windows are at best useless and at worst an impediment to furniture placement and optimum use. Positioned too high or too low, windows may be likened to ill-fitting clothing, either too constraining or unsuitably large.

Windows give us light and frame a scene outside the home. While lots of windows may seem desirable when you look at a floor plan, remember to consider what the view through them will be. Will a neighbor's house be too close? Will a street scene be annoying at night because headlights disrupt your tranquillity? An architect should be able to help you visualize what you'll be seeing by drawing small sketches of views from the various windows in each room. If your lot is empty, stand in the middle and take photographs in all directions to have a record of all the views from the house.

Just as important as the view can be the relation of the windows to the furniture in a room. This might mean simply putting your furniture in a different place than you had envisioned it, or it may mean rethinking window placement when you're building or remodeling. Again, be sure you know what will fit where.

There are some places that feng shui dictates are always inappropriate spots for windows: directly behind a bed; too high on the wall for you to see out from your bed, office chair, or dining room table; and directly behind a seating area, as shown in Figure 4.10. Any window whose view is obscured while seated or standing, typically a window placed above standing eye level, can reduce feelings of connection and compromise safety by offering exposure without in turn revealing what is outside.

I remember standing with a family on their recently purchased lot on which the foundation had just been poured. Pointing out the adverse placement of sliding glass doors on the floor plan, I asked them to imagine themselves sitting on the sofa in the yet-to-be-built room and picture the scene framed by the sliders. They quickly realized that a stately oak tree that they had had transplanted from another location at great expense would not be visible without moving the sliding glass doors about one foot to one side. You may not be able to command an idyllic view from every window in your home, but you can often adjust a plan so that the view doesn't annoy you. How many times have you seen a window that framed a neighbor's air-conditioning unit or bathroom window? The following list will tell you which views are most likely to keep you from using different rooms for their intended purpose.

Inappropriate Window Placement and Views to Watch For
- In gathering spaces: avoid views of blank walls, other living spaces, utility areas, or parking spaces
- In bedrooms: avoid windows that frame a neighbor's bedroom or gathering space window; as shown in Figure 4.11, avoid placing windows behind the bed, which deters a feeling of security
- In children's bedrooms: avoid views of the driveway or roads, especially if there is a traffic light or stop sign, which could be construed as an area of access by strangers
- In dining rooms: avoid viewing a neighbor's backyard or a busy street, which are possible distractions

Figure 4.10 People facing those seated at the sofa will no longer be distracted now that the windows have been reconfigured.

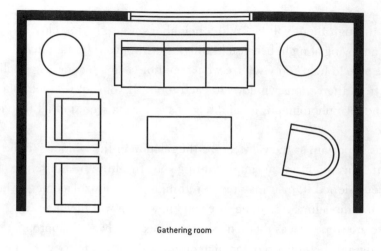

Gathering room

a. Poor window placement for the furniture arrangement

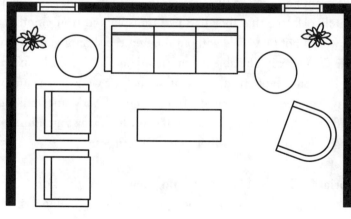

Gathering room

b. Better window placement for furniture arrangement

- In home offices: avoid facing a blank wall or positioning a window too high to permit a view when seated
- In bathrooms: avoid positioning windows directly across from any neighbor's window or an outdoor gathering space
- In any room: avoid having a window frame a view that you find disturbing (may include cemeteries, hospitals, schools, and religious institutions)

With these points in mind, ask yourself the questions in the following sections.

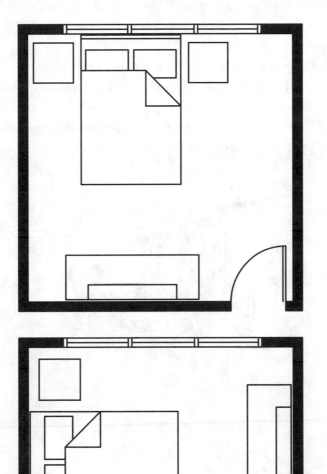

a. Before

b. After

Figure 4.11 Moving the bed to a solid wall with a side view of the windows provides the same light as if the bed were in front of the window, but is a more relaxing position.

Will People Likely Be Standing or Sitting in a Space?

Appropriate window size, height, and placement in a particular room is a combination of practical factors as well as personal preference and the outdoor scenery. First ask yourself how the room will be used and what furniture will be in it. In general, windows should be placed so that eye level is at the midpoint of the opening. To determine where a window should be, you have to know whether the people looking out it will be sitting or standing, as captured in Figure 4.12. This means the appropriate window placement is higher in hallways than in dining rooms. Sometimes, however, you may want to position a window much higher than the rule of thumb dictates. For example, you may want to sacrifice the ability to look out while still allowing light to enter so that privacy is assured.

Hallways are perfect examples of spaces that need views at standing height. Kitchens, on the other hand, have some areas where people sit and some where they stand. In bedrooms and dining rooms, people are more likely to spend time seated. If a window is to provide a view rather than simply admit light, its location on the wall is important. Figure 4.13 illustrates how to place windows to frame action.

Figure 4.12 Window size and height should be linked to whether the space is typically used sitting or standing.

Figure 4.13 Raise (a) or lower (b) window placement based on the appropriateness of view. Should the scene be distracting, a higher one would be appropriate, or if the scene is tranquil and appropriate, the lower one will suit the space.

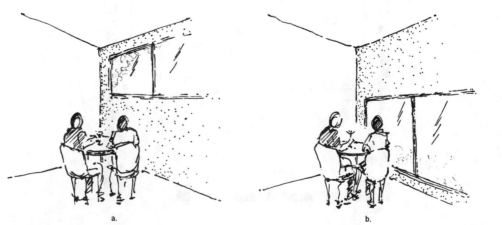

a.   b.

If a window's view seems inappropriate and you don't have the option of placing it on a different wall, there are many ways to camouflage or tone down a negative view. As illustrated in Figures 4.14 and 4.15, corner windows, clerestory windows, portholes, and skylights may solve the problem, as might placing fences or trellises outside the window.

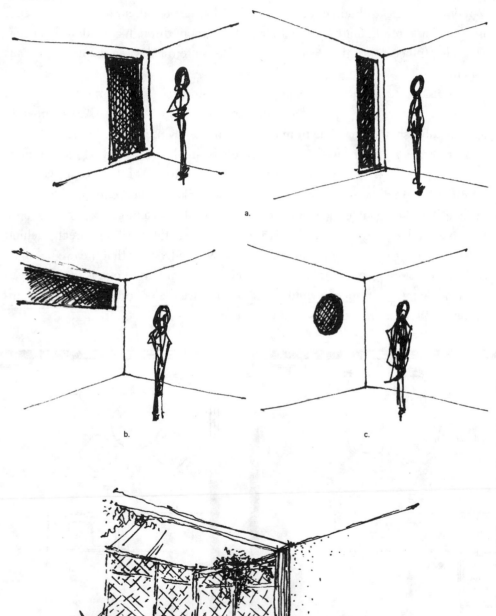

a.

b.   c.

Figure 4.14 (a) Well-placed windows can resolve the need for light while hiding inappropriate views. (b) Ribbon windows placed above standing sight line ensure privacy while permitting light and a sky or treetop view. (c) Sometimes a snippet of window is just perfect to frame a partial view while leaving plenty of wall space for artwork and decoration.

Figure 4.15 Installing a trellis outside can alter a large window framing a neighbor's home or an unsightly scene.

As to children's bedrooms, it's not so much what the child will see as what the child will imagine is on the other side of the window that you need to take into account. Children typically occupy a home's smaller bedrooms, and therefore window placement is critical to the ultimate position of a bed. A child's bed should be placed at right angles to a window and not in front of it. The reasoning is very simple. Windows can make children feel vulnerable. Monsters or other creatures of fanciful imagination often figuratively penetrate a child's room through a window. Like closets and entrance doors, the placement of windows is critical when shaping bedrooms for children.

The same reasoning applies to adult bedrooms, save for the monster part. As human beings, we have a primal and instinctive need to feel safe. Any area perceived as vulnerable should be visible from the most frequently used place in the room, and conversely any area perceived as private should be hidden from view at the entrance.

In Figure 4.16 the sink was repositioned to take advantage of the existing windows, for often cooking is a solo activity whose sense of isolation can be reduced by a view outside. The dining table and chairs were repositioned from a more conventional position to one askew in order to mitigate the windows' negative positions directly behind two of the diners. From a feng shui perspective, we understand that the eye naturally seeks light before form; therefore, in the new configuration no one is under viewed by being directly in front of a window. All diners have the opportunity to enjoy natural light and, if desired, easily seek a view outside.

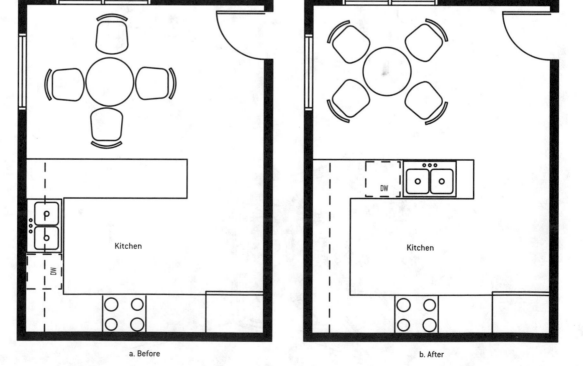

Figure 4.16 The sink area, the most frequently used place in this homeowner's kitchen, was repositioned to face the seating area and picture window beyond it. Notice how the chairs are off square in the dining area, providing the cook a better direct view of that space.

a. Before

b. After

I have friends whose bedroom faced the ocean, but the window was positioned too high up for them to enjoy the view while in bed. By replacing this window with one that permitted a view of the ocean from the bed, they found that they used their bedroom far more than before and admitted the feature improved their romantic life. When a room's use and its windows are well integrated, it functions gracefully.

Additionally, bear in mind that what is good for an elderly person might be a teenager's downfall. In planning an assisted-care facility, I asked my client to situate the facility close to an active area like a schoolyard or park. The activity generated in those places is a lifeline for those whose physical movements are curtailed. However that same scene could be a major distraction for a teenager's study area. What is an elixir for one group could be another's poison. Take the occupant's personality, emotional needs, and cultural conditioning into consideration when you choose a window's view.

THE EFFECTS OF WINDOW VIEWS ON DIFFERENT PEOPLE

Scene	Detriment to	Beneficial to
Street	Teenagers when studying or dining	Those living alone
Neighbor's dwellings	Those easily distracted	Those feeling lonely
Expanses of lawn	Those in a sick room or where activities need stimulus	When calm is necessary
Flowers	Detriment only if uncared for	When optimism is needed
Traffic light	Families spending too few hours together	Those requiring change

---

Where Will Your Windows Cast Natural Light?

The time of day a room is in use also influences the position of windows. For example, if a gathering room's windows face west and everybody gathers there at dusk, it is reasonable to consider whether the setting sun will be a factor that influences family activities. If the horizon is flat and there are no obstructions, the setting sun's glare might interfere with reading and relaxing. If buildings, vegetation, or mountains prevent the sun from shining directly into a room, the day's final glow might comfort or relax its occupants.

Remember that outside light does not reach across an entire room unless the windows are high and the ceilings are high and light colored. In Figure 4.17 the bay windows demonstrate how to light a work area and lessen the feeling of being closed in

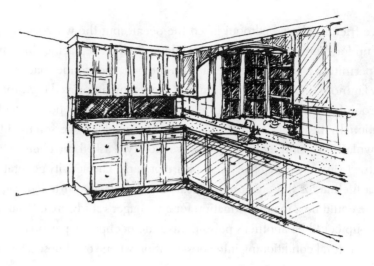

Figure 4.17 These large kitchen windows over the sink provide illumination in daytime as well as a depth view for the cook.

while facing a wall. Standard windows will permit direct sunlight to penetrate only about three to four feet toward a room's center; its intensity will be reduced greatly from that point on. When analyzing a floor plan, use a colored highlighter to fill in the circle of light coming from each window. It will help you immensely to uncover a room's daytime brightness. Knowing how far daylight will reach can make a great difference in your planning of furniture placement, especially desks, couches, beds, and reading chairs.

How Should Windows Open?

Since her living room's windows were on the only suitable wall for her couch, my aunt Estelle had to climb onto the couch every time she needed to open her windows to let in the fresh air. These large windows had yet another problematic feature: they faced west. The sun's blinding afternoon glare crisscrossed the faces of family members, making them blink and grimace while they talked. Drawing the curtains plunged the room into an eerie premature nighttime and was never considered an alternative. My aunt's living room windows were simply in the wrong place.

The need to have windows that open easily over a kitchen sink seems obvious, yet many of us have experienced how difficult this simple act can be. The fact that these windows need frequent cleaning because of cooking vapors and kitchen grease makes it even more critical to have our kitchen windows within easy reach.

Bedroom windows should be secure yet easy to manipulate. Horror stories of children falling from windows evokes mental images of windows placed either too low or too wide on the wall. A family that I advised who lived on a small Greek island had low, peephole-size windows installed in the children's bedroom. These tiny windows provided visual access to the stunning view while protecting the children, who spent a lot of time playing on the floor.

Figure 4.18 contains a chart of different window types. Think through exactly what is needed to make a space fit the intended activities and then consider what windows can fulfill this intention best.

How Much Wall Space Should a Window Occupy?

Be sure you consider whether the room will be used primarily during the day or at night before you select window sizes. On the surface larger seems better, but too many large windows may impose a lot of limitations on where you put furniture and how you decorate the room. If the room is used mainly during the dark, you may be better off with smaller or fewer windows. We have a colleague who lives in a cozy older home in upstate New York, shown in Figure 4.19. The living room is in the center of the home with only one wall contiguous to the outside. That wall is pivotal to the home's entrance and the path to the staircase. Therefore, the window's benefit exists mostly for the threshold and pathway space. While there are openings in the walls that permit light to filter in from surrounding rooms (because the owner has a three-sided sunroom for daytime use), the main seating section of this room is darker than most gathering spaces. But since this room is used mostly during the evening, the scarcity of windows does not lessen the room's appeal or use.

Windows as Furniture

When seating is furnished in a room's center rather than at the perimeter, window seats can contribute to the room's flexibility. Dining rooms, gathering rooms, bedrooms, and kitchens are good candidates for window seats. In a large room, window seats can provide getaway spaces for one or two persons. In small rooms, window seats add extra seating and also create an alternative intimate space. As little as a couple of square feet is all that's needed of a room's floor area to accommodate a window seat.

Artificial Lighting

Lighting is probably the greatest challenge to visualize when you look at a floor plan. If either too much or not enough light in a room has ever been annoying, the importance of a light's position has been demonstrated. A ceiling light symbol will not tell you how much light you will have to read the fine print of a contract or the notes on a sheet of music. Try to become familiar with lighting fixtures and their wattage, as

Figure 4.18 This chart allows you to compare the pros and cons of various window styles.

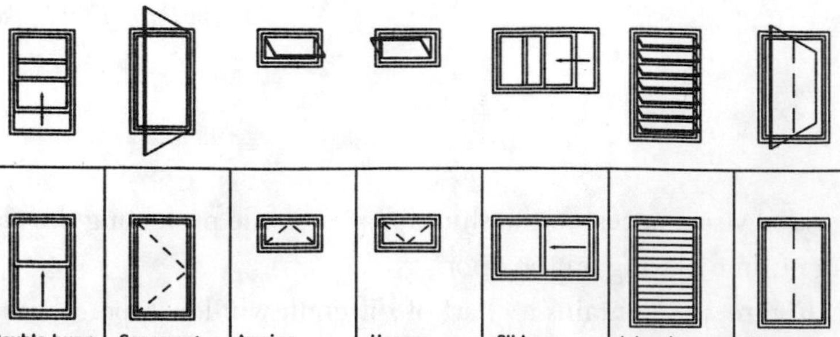

	Fixed	Double-hung	Casement	Awning	Hopper	Slide	Jalousie	Pivot
		Slides open vertically	Swings open from side	Opens from the bottom out	Opens from the top in	Slides open horizontally	Multiple glass slats open from the top out	Pivots open from center
Positive Characteristics								
Not likely to sag	●	●		●	●	●		●
Easy installation of screen & storm sash		●		●	●	●		
Provides 100% vent opening			●	●	●		●	●
Easy to wash		●			●		●	●
Deflects drafts			●	●	●		●	●
Offers rain protection, partly open				●	●		●	
Diverts inflowing air upward				●	●		●	
Odd sizes economically available						●	●	
Large sizes practical	●					●		
Negative Characteristics								
Only 50% of area openable		●				●		
Doesn't protect from rain when open		●	●			●		●
Inconvenient to use if over obstruction		●				●		
Hazardous if low vent next to walk			●					
Horizontal members obstruct view		●					●	
Vertical members obstruct view			●			●		
Will sag if not structurally strong			●					
Glass quickly soils when vent open				●	●		●	●
Inflowing air cannot be diverted down		●	●	●	●	●	●	
Excessive air leakage hard to wash							●	
Interferes with furniture, window treatments, etc.					●			●
Difficult to provide screens/storm sash						●		●
Hard to wash							●	

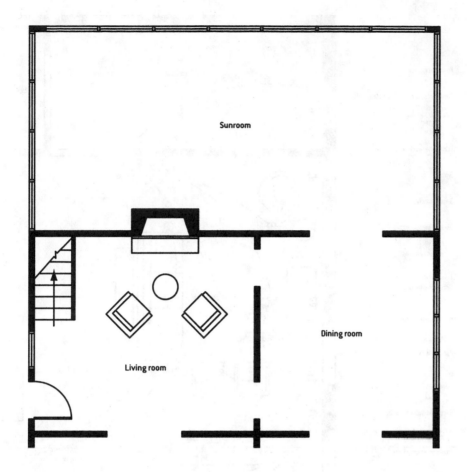

Figure 4.19 Sometimes windows are not pertinent to a room's use. In this home the window appropriately lit the passageway but not the seated area.

relevant to your space. The variables that influence the amount of light that reaches a surface are:

- The height of a ceiling
- The angle or source the light is pitched from
- Wall and floor colors and textures
- The number and type of reflective surfaces in the space

If a room has ceiling fixtures, then the cone of light cast should fall appropriately over the room's furnishings, table surfaces, or the paths leading to the areas of use in the room. Figure 4.20 shows how the cones of light should be located according to the room's use and furniture layout.

Different activities within a space affect how the light should be positioned. Plan on lighting that will illuminate each activity you are likely to engage in at the appropriate angle and with sufficient wattage. This type of lighting is called "task lighting."

Activities to Consider When Planning Task Lighting
- Doing something at a table
- Holding reading material like a book or newspaper at an angle

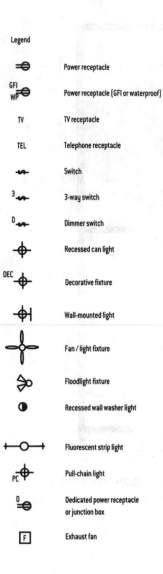

Legend

⊝	Power receptacle
GFI WP ⊝	Power receptacle (GFI or waterproof)
TV	TV receptacle
TEL	Telephone receptacle
∿	Switch
3∿	3-way switch
D∿	Dimmer switch
✛	Recessed can light
DEC ✛	Decorative fixture
✛	Wall-mounted light
✤	Fan / light fixture
⋋	Floodlight fixture
◑	Recessed wall washer light
⊢○⊣	Fluorescent strip light
PC ✛	Pull-chain light
D ⊝	Dedicated power receptacle or junction box
F	Exhaust fan

Figure 4.20 This chart of common electrical symbols will help you understand a floor plan's lighting. Place your furniture in your floor plan so as to position lighting appropriately.

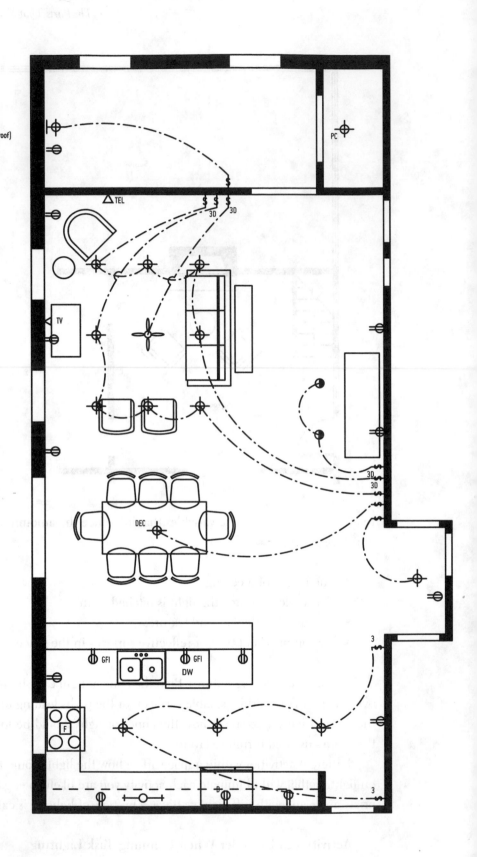

- Knitting or sewing
- Staring at a computer screen
- Looking at a large surface or focusing on a small one

Also take into account how long you are likely to be at a particular task in one sitting. The longer it takes to accomplish a task, the more light is needed.

If imagining doing these tasks does not help you choose the right lighting to install, consider holding a clip-on light in different positions until a particular angle and wattage seems right. Lighting is best conceived with a concept of furniture placement in mind so that the activities can be illuminated appropriately.

Lighting in transition areas such as stairs and hallways is also important to consider early in the planning stage. This type of lighting is called "ambient lighting." When considering ambient lighting, think of how movement through a space would benefit from illumination. For example, you should be able to turn on a light at the threshold of the staircase. It will add measurably to a feeling of security when, for example, switches are placed outside each bedroom to light the bottom and top of the staircase. Figure 4.21 shows the connection between wall switches and the lights they engage.

To illustrate how important it is to know exactly which switch will turn on a certain light, let me share a past experience. A builder contacted me to feng shui a model home. The development was designed for couples who would take part in many leisure activities. However, it is well known that age reduces visual acuity and that as you age you need more, not less, light. This particular floor plan had a light switch next to the

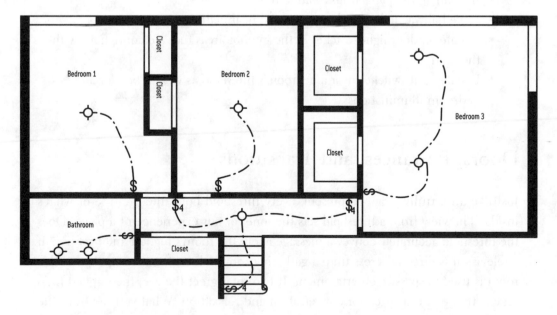

Figure 4.21 The lines from the wall to the middle of the ceiling show which switches control which ceiling lights.

entrance that engaged only one ceiling light directly above the entrance. Once the occupants moved forward, they were literally in the dark. The hallway extended from the small entrance area through the center of the home, and all rooms spread out from it. However, walking down the hall, it was necessary to switch on lights along the way to see where you were going. This daily annoyance would certainly not be good feng shui, for feng shui suggests that one should flow through a home as naturally as water flows across a rock. The remedy was simple and didn't add one cent to the builder's expenses. Connecting all hallway-ceiling lights to the foyer's switch made it easy to illuminate the entire pathway leading to every area of the home.

Be sure to distinguish task lighting from path lighting as shown in Figure 4.22, and consider the importance of both. Be sure that easily accessed lighting illuminates the room's most important function. Perhaps if the room shown in Figure 4.22 was a frequently used gathering space it would need three switches to be lit appropriately and conveniently.

Most municipal codes governing lighting and electrical work are structured to promote the safety and well-being of a building's occupants. While these codes should always be met, we encourage you to think about your spaces beyond what is simply required. As a building inspector we know once quipped, "These codes really have nothing to do with logic." Keeping this in mind, please review the following list.

Lighting Considerations to Make Living Easier
- Have light switches near entrance doors lighting the path to use areas.
- Include electrical outlets or built-in lighting near logical use areas.
- Illuminate the paths from room to room.
- Have hallway light switches positioned near bedrooms.
- Locate outdoor light switches in the interior areas that are contiguous with the light.
- Locate light switches near a bedroom's threshold as well as bed for all bedroom illuminations.

Doors, Entrances, and Transitions

Just like an artfully wrapped present, every threshold holds the promise of what's inside. The view from a threshold sets the tone for our experience of a place. Does the threshold accurately convey a message about the room's highest and best use? If a television is directly across from a gathering room's door, the message is that this room is used for passive entertainment. If two sofas greet the eye, the implied message is that this is a space for conversation and relaxation. What you see from the

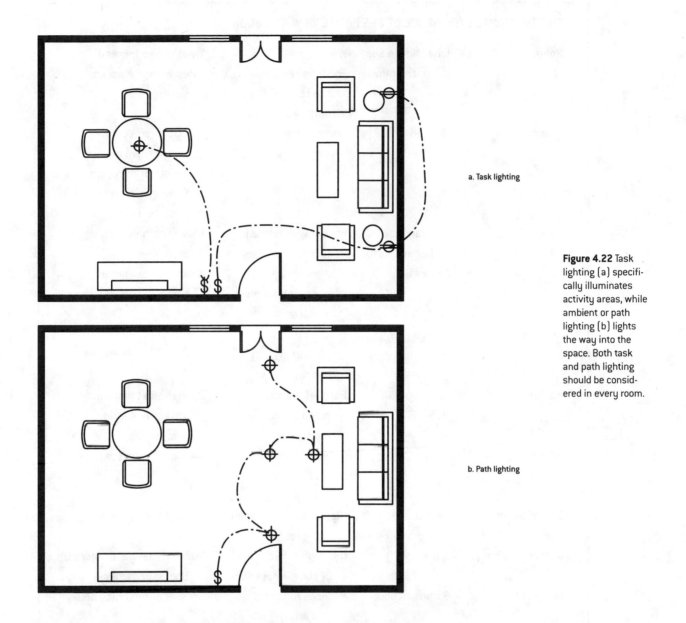

a. Task lighting

b. Path lighting

Figure 4.22 Task lighting (a) specifically illuminates activity areas, while ambient or path lighting (b) lights the way into the space. Both task and path lighting should be considered in every room.

entrance to a room often reflects what you will do there. Therefore, be sure the view from the threshold appropriately expresses your expectations for the space.

Thresholds can be open or shielded by doors, and which a room has will affect the perception of the room as people enter it. Doorways reveal a space slowly, image by image, while open entrances expose the space in front of you more forthrightly. When you stand at a threshold or a door, consider how the room reveals itself to you and if your first impression is appropriate to the room's functioning. The list on page 94 shows which views might have an undesirable effect.

Consider what a threshold communicates and determine if it is beneficial to the space's activities and your specific requirements. If a room has several entrances, eval-

THE EMOTIONAL EXPERIENCE OF THE INITIAL VIEW OF A ROOM

Room	What Not to See	Why	What to See Instead
Foyer	Oversized mirror	Focuses person on the self, not the setting	A destination such as seating
Foyer	Kitchen	Encourages overeating	A visual representation of a positive activity (photo of the occupants fishing, running a marathon, skiing, etc.)
Foyer	Hallway to bedroom	Encourages retreating to private spaces	A loved common activity area
Foyer	An exit door	May encourage passing through a space	A pathway to another common gathering area
Kitchen	Refrigerator	Focuses person on consuming, not creating	Cookbooks
Kitchen	Sink	Focuses person on preparation, not results	Open cabinet displaying attractive serving pieces
Kitchen	Stove	Focuses person on waiting, not performing	Rack of pots and pans
Gathering room	Back of seating units	Distances person from using room	Facing seating
Gathering room	Television	Diminishes likelihood of social interaction	Built-ins that house stereo, books, or games
Couple's bedroom	Bathroom door	Reduces romantic quality	Dresser or grooming area
Couple's bedroom	Television	Distracts from intimate closeness	Bed as main focus
Children's bedroom	Door to outside	Fosters insecurity	A built-in with favorite toys or objects
Bathroom	Window behind toilet	Compromises complete relaxation	Shelf displaying notions
Bathroom	Toilet	Increases vulnerability when using	Vanity
Dining room	Activity center	Discourages lingering at table	Well-tended central display on table

uate the one used most frequently, whether or not it is the architectural threshold of the room. For example, should the gathering room be seen mostly when family members exit the bedroom hallway, make sure what they see from that entrance is the main part of the gathering space, not a far-distant hall or kitchen area.

Choosing a Door or an Opening

In our culture, doors are normally installed to provide privacy and shield an area from public view. Almost without exception, bedrooms and bathrooms are accessed through a door. Kitchens, however, normally open up to gathering or dining spaces. While that is convenient, it often permits a view into a kitchen that may not always be beneficial. Figures 4.23 and 4.24 give some options to consider if the view of an interior space is unacceptable to the dining or entertaining area.

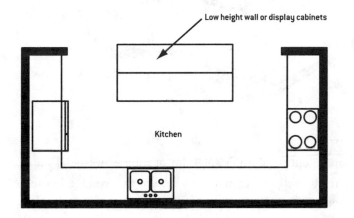

Low height wall or display cabinets

Kitchen

Figure 4.23 A raised counter hides a potentially messy workspace but allows the cook to remain part of the adjacent activity.

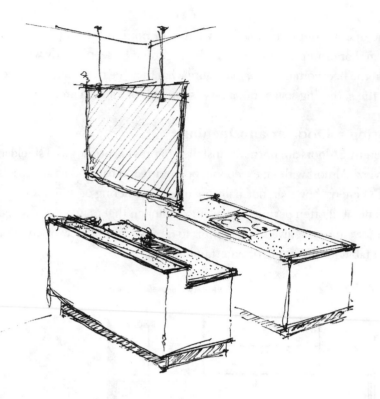

Figure 4.24 Artwork can hide unsightliness and a track for a painting can be an inventive way to conceal a kitchen's mess.

Double or Single Doors

Double doors for a home's main entrance imply splendor or interest in social status, which does not necessarily relate well to a casual lifestyle. For the average house, a double door raises expectations of formality and may appear so pompous and intimidating that guests feel slightly ill at ease. Is the message you care to promote really that of double doors, better suited for grand mansions, museums, and churches? Figure 4.25 is a sketch of a home with a rather formal and imposing entryway, especially incongruous in the rather modest neighborhood in which the house is located.

Appropriate Widths for Different Doorways

Consider how people will likely enter the space and make sure the entry width is appropriate. Today a door clearance of thirty-two inches is a minimum standard for wheelchair accessibility. This is the minimum desirable width for all doors that lead from area to area and room to room. However, common spaces are often better served when the threshold is wide enough to let two people enter side by side. A den/study/hideaway would benefit from a double-width entrance that can be closed, whereas the entrance to a kitchen might benefit from a Dutch door (see Figure 4.26), where the top and bottom can be closed separately to hide any disarray. In addition to the traditional use of a Dutch door to lead to the outside, consider using them in

Figure 4.25 Over-sized entrance doors exude a formality not necessarily appropriate for a family home, which would be better served by communicating a cozy sense of place.

Figure 4.26 Dutch doors allow flexibility of visual and auditory access to common areas.

locations that could benefit from improved air flow ventilation or the restriction of visual access. In the same way that spices enhance food, a variety of thresholds enhance each room.

Individualizing Doors

Imbue each door with individuality. On a visit to a small monastery on a Greek island I noticed a door with a head mounted above the knob. Just as a nameplate would signify the ownership of an office or home, this was a replica of the occupant's face and in my mind artfully indicated the room's inhabitant. Consider how each door can communicate the unique characteristic of the room or the personality of its user.

A simple hook can be mounted to display a three-dimensional artifact or two-dimensional picture. Many years ago, when I was lecturing on feng shui at the national convention of the American Institute of Architects, one of the other speakers described how sturdy hooks had been installed on the underside of the support beams of the porticoes in a low-income townhouse project. And, indeed, soon after moving in, the residents had used the hooks to hang their unique artifacts such as flags and birdhouses—even bicycles. The personalized entrances gave the public project precisely the community and family feel the architects had envisioned.

Consider a variety of knobs, trim, and styles to individualize the interior doors of your home. Bedroom doors could be styled with many details if they are located in a featureless hallway. Bathroom doors should be different from closet or bedroom doors and give some hint of the room's use. If changing doors is not an option, alter the surroundings of the doors. Doors enclosed by bookshelves arouse interest and curiosity. Light and shadows cast on a door's surface make it more appealing.

Rules of Thumb for Doors
- Bathroom doors should not be seen from seating or sleeping areas. In Figure 4.27a the bathroom door is within clear view of the bed, and the toilet can be seen when the door is open.
- Make sure the bathroom door doesn't swing open in a direction that will reveal its interior to the seating or gathering area, as it does in Figure 4.27b.
- Doors into a main gathering area should open to reveal the room, not a brief view of the adjacent wall, as shown in Figure 4.27c.
- When you enter a room, there should be no wall that blocks more than half the room's view, as there is in Figure 4.27d.

Footpaths and Eye Paths

As discussed in Chapter 1, plazas, a feature in many European cities, typically have roads like spokes in a wheel's hub. All roads lead to the center and like a magnet draw a city's inhabitants to these public gathering spaces. In the same way, as many interior pathways as possible should guide the inhabitants of a home to its heart. Typically,

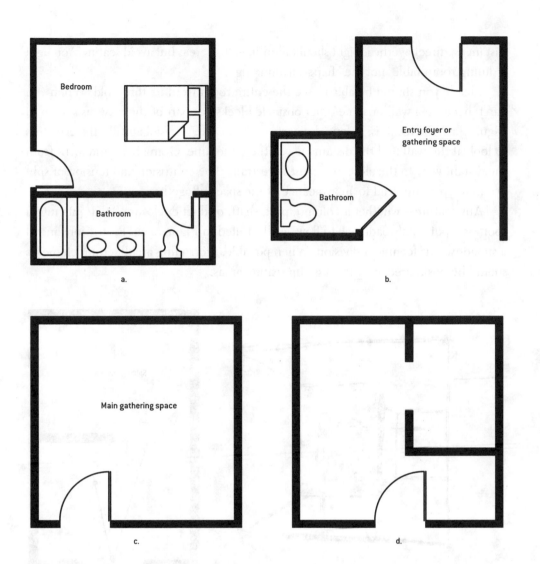

Figure 4.27 Doors with poor feng shui. (a) It is best not to see inside a bathroom from bed, but should this be impossible, at least the toilet should not be visible from bed when the bathroom door is opened. (b) Remember that the swing of a bathroom door should not reveal its interior to the areas of use in adjoining rooms. In general, locate toilets out of view from the threshold of any bathroom. (c) An entrance door should swing open so that the main area of a room is not blocked. (d) The view from a doorway should frame one scene, not split the eye between the close-up wall and the distance view. In feng shui this is called a split eye.

though, great attention is already given to room-to-room connections—hallways, stairs, and passageways. Just as much attention should be given to moving through each individual room.

Wherever you go, your eyes get there before your body. Therefore, pathways should be considered first visually, then physically. Specifically, this means that a pathway through a room should be visually easy to identify, appropriately pleasing, and easy to negotiate from a logical beginning to its end. To be sure your building or remodeling project yields this result, conceive the furniture layout of each and every room ahead of time. The routes from a sofa to a stereo, a bookshelf, or a game table are some of the interroom passages to consider.

One way to accentuate pathways is to provide them with down lighting. The eye seeks light instinctively; therefore proper lighting will accentuate passageways. In all instances, direct overhead light should illuminate use areas but avoid seating. You light a dining room table, not the chairs surrounding it.

Ideally you should be able to see the entire room from its threshold. When you can't, because a wall or some other obstacle blocks out part of the view, as shown in Figure 4.28, the result is, in feng shui terms, a "split eye." Physiologically, the eye seeks to look at the wall and the distant view at the same time. Going back and forth from the distant view to the close one causes eyestrain. The confusion and tension of split eye may over time lead to an avoidance of the space altogether.

Any feature—whether a column, post, shaft, or duct enclosure—that juts into a room is a potential roadblock to flow, as illustrated in Figure 4.29. Protrusions instill a subconscious feeling of division. When possible, protruding architectural elements should be positioned away from group seating areas.

Figure 4.28 When we see both a depth view and a close-up wall, confusion and tension are our first experiences when entering a space.

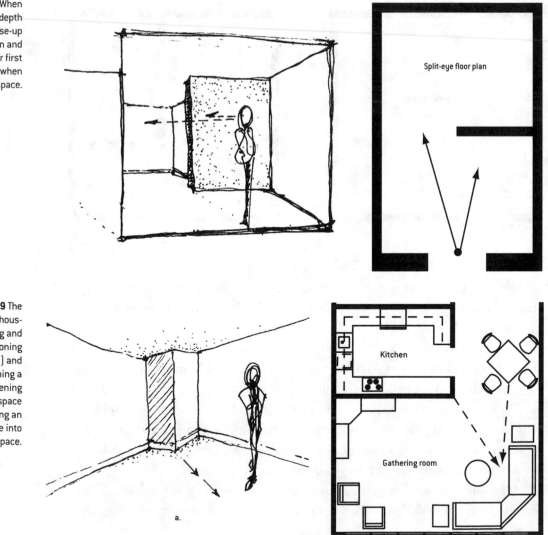

Figure 4.29 The protrusions housing heating and air-conditioning ductwork (a) and edges defining a room opening (b) divide a space by projecting an obstacle into the space.

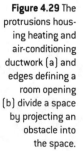

In L-shaped spaces, the corner of the exposed wall is a potential flow inhibitor. In feng shui, any two walls that come together at a sharp angle projecting an experiential line into the space is referred to as a "secret arrow." However, positioning doors diagonally at the confluence of right angles, as we did in Figure 4.30, will make the entrance more integral to the entire radius of surrounding space. This unusually positioned door integrates the two spaces and averts the sharp edge or secret arrow. Plants, screens, and round pedestals holding artwork can camouflage secret arrows as well.

Appropriately Pleasing Pathways

Hallways connecting bedrooms are often drab and dull. If they are more than seven steps long, they are good candidates for architectural diversity. Consider niches, protected narrow shelving, or alternate use of materials to make traveling down a long passageway pleasing, as demonstrated in Figure 4.31.

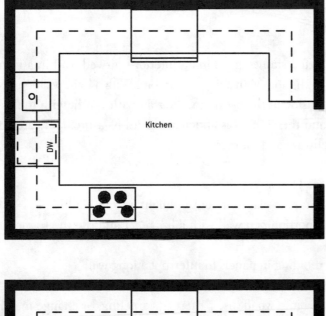

a.

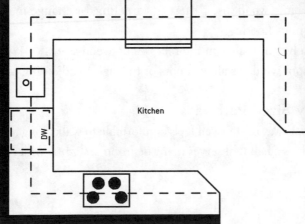

b.

Figure 4.30 This room's constrained feel (a) is improved, as is the cook's visual access, by changing the doorway. The diagonal entrance (b) better integrates the room with the adjacent gathering space.

Figure 4.31 Hallways can become striking when a flat wall is perforated with niches to house sculptures, books, or artwork.

I once inserted stained glass in an interior stairwell wall in a former residence. The wall was contiguous with a guest bedroom. With a light positioned on the stained glass from the inside of the bedroom, the stair path was lit with the dazzling glow of colored glass and the climb was anticipated with pleasure. Here are a few choices to consider in hallways and stairways.

Options for Hallways
- Install a stained-glass window and light it from behind.
- Frame a portion of a wall with a bas-relief and use the frame to highlight artwork.
- Attach molding in panels to interrupt a long wall.
- Drape undulating cloths over dowels on a long narrow ceiling.
- Insert tiles into wood, use patterned carpeting, or change materials to break up contiguous flooring.
- Create shelves or niches in the recesses between studs.
- Add transom windows above doors or through to adjoining rooms.

Appropriately Sized Pathways

A standard-size pathway or stairwell feels comfortable to walk along alone, but in high-traffic areas, such as a hall that serves many bedrooms, slightly wider passageways that allow two people to pass each other comfortably will prevent a lot of irritation. Where is it written that hallways have to be long rectangular tunnels? Hallway walls can have sections recessed to hold shelves or narrow cupboards sufficiently wide for such items as sewing materials, toiletries, hammers, screwdrivers, tape, pencils, paper, or wine. A door recessed in this way provides a sense of privacy for such rooms as bathrooms, bedrooms, or home offices.

Command Positions

In feng shui, the term "command position" is the location in a room that commands the most attention from the threshold. Those seated in the command position of a room are imbued with more authority than are those in other locations. When you stand at the threshold of a room, what and whom you see in the command position will determine how you will experience the room. So will what you see from the command position. A family unit is often served best when the person viewed as the head of the household occupies the command position.

The most important command position is the space facing the entrance on the farthest wall; it is the spot where thrones are typically placed. However, all seating has the potential to be commanding as long as windows are not positioned behind it. Figure 4.32 shows how the rearrangement of furnishings can alter a space to put all seating in a command position.

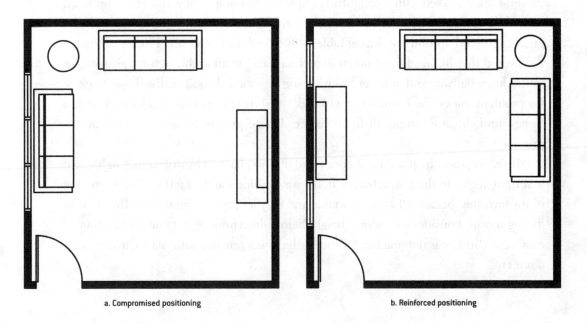

a. Compromised positioning   b. Reinforced positioning

Figure 4.32
Replacing one large picture window (a) that distracted this room's command position with separate windows (b) afforded this gathering space a better command position.

What should be in the command position depends most on what the room's purpose is. If it is not to foster interactive conversation, it's fine to put a window on the wall directly opposite and farthest from the entrance. The following table shows other things that could be in the command position of different spaces.

WHAT CAN BE PLACED IN THE COMMAND POSITION	
Room or Space	**Command Position**
Entrance hall	View to main gathering space or pathway leading to it
Hallway	Wall niche or artwork
Gathering space	Sofa or chair used by the "head of the family"
Kitchen	The most well-used cooking area
Bathroom	Sink or vanity
Bedroom	Bed (in this case away from entrance's center)
Library	Reading chair
Television room	Largest seating unit

Potential Distractions

Movement distracts. Distracting views behind a command position can dissipate its power. I once worked with a delightful couple whose complaint was that the husband was often ignored when they entertained—though this was not the case when the guests gathered around the dining table, at the pool, or in the small library. When I discovered that he liked to sit down in a chair backing an archway through which a rather large hallway and another room sprang into view, I soon realized the cause of his problem. Since the human eye will seek the distant view before it focuses on the foreground, he was simply difficult to see; hence people tended to overlook his presence.

If seating must be placed in a command position backed by distracting sights, put it at right angles to the distraction or find a way to hide the distraction. Plants are one of my favorites, because they are portable and they let dappled light shine through. In dining rooms, consider a window's height before determining if it adds distraction. If moving a window is not practical, conceal the lower portion with plants, artifacts, or a screen.

When we sit in a command position with our back to a window, hallway, or moving object, our concentration is disrupted because we instinctively remain vigilant to who or what might approach from the rear. Sound-producing flooring in passageways behind a seating arrangement will help solve this problem by providing advance warning of another person's approach.

Compassion Territories

Compassion territories are spaces that exude comfort. In pyramid feng shui, the right side of an entrance is considered the compassion space. Since the majority of people tend to be right-side dominant and since most of us pause upon entering a room, objects placed to the right of an entrance will communicate the degree of care that can be expected. A sturdy table or shelf or any surface where we can rest our hand or put down whatever we may carry with us generally suffices. Shelves or niches for keys, gloves, or a hat are necessary to lend comfort to the compassion area at a home's entrance. In gathering spaces, providing storage space for items frequently used to the right of the entrance can satisfy inhabitants' needs. A wall with built-in shelving will serve not only as a sturdy piece of furniture but also as a compassion area. What to avoid are doorways to other areas, low windows, or closets.

Architecturally it is important that unused wall space or a feature that serves as a place for depositing or retrieving articles be to the right of the threshold of each room, as it is in Figure 4.33.

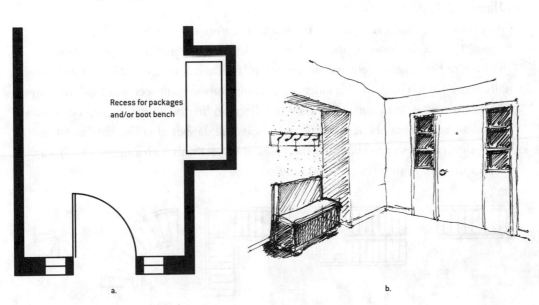

Recess for packages and/or boot bench

a.

b.

Figure 4.33 (a) A compassion niche is created when there are objects or features serving the needs of those who enter a space. (b) In this front entrance of an active young family's home, compassion is served by coat hooks and a bench for taking off shoes.

Staircases Without Turns

Scaling a mountain by spiraling upward is far easier than attempting a straight vertical ascent. When conceiving of a stairway, then, design it with at least one bend. Figure 4.34 shows the options to consider other than a straight staircase.

Spiral staircases are, however, best avoided. Gyrating in a circle is unnatural, gives rise to dizziness, and inhibits the rhythm of movement from floor to floor. In our homes, we don't need the thrill of carnival rides spinning us around while catapulting us through space. Curved stairs, on the other hand, can be a graceful and relaxed way to climb upstairs.

Threatening Chi

Large, inappropriately close, or imposingly high features make us feel diminished and less powerful. Nancilee's son grew to six feet, four inches in his teens. Grown men and women deferred to him in a way that adults don't normally do to other, less imposing teens. Height and might go together. When large, imposing features are designed into a home they can reduce the inhabitant's sense of power. In religious institutions, for example, a raised dais with imposing features in a great volume of space appropriately helps us remove vestiges of our egos and self-will.

In feng shui, we call inappropriately sized features "sha chi," or threatening chi. To avoid having threatening chi in your home, consider the scale of not only the architectural features, but also of the proximity of large furnishings to the likely placement of people in a space.

Diagonal Lines

Our eyes notice diagonal lines and large objects before other shapes and sizes. In our genesis, this visual discrimination helped us survive. Diagonal lines require two calculations of both the descent and the trajectory. Furthermore, large objects are potentially more threatening than smaller ones. Consider the nanosecond of calculation that might cost an ancestor's life should the diagonal line be a tiger leaping out from behind a tree. Diagonal lines also suggest a potential danger of falling such as a leaning tree or a steep slope. Therefore staircases or a short wall with a diagonal line can keep us inappropriately tuned in to danger.

Figure 4.34 Staircases can bend, be separated by a landing, or curve.

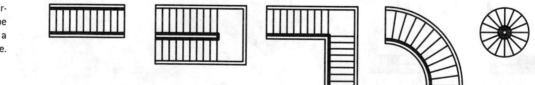

Lighting fixtures and their placement sometimes send ominous messages. Large lighting fixtures in small places may seem menacing, especially when placed on stairwells or narrow passages where an alternative escape route doesn't exist. The light from ceiling fixtures that cast a diagonal shadow across a furniture grouping can create subtle threatening lines. Remember, all lighting from a single source creates a feeling of darkness outside the direct circle of illumination. Thus lamps, spotlights, and other fixtures that direct the light downward have the potential to draw attention away from other areas in a room. Therefore it is best to plan ceiling light so that it casts overlapping cones of light, to avoid an abrupt shadow stretching to the next cone of light. Should you sometimes want dramatic or specific ceiling lighting, have different lights attached to separate on/off switches.

Architects and builders are trained to visualize what structures will look like and how they will serve their functions before they are built. Most homeowners don't have that skill. But it's far easier and cheaper to adjust sizes, change window heights and door swings, and rearrange lighting in the planning stage than following construction. Learning to use floor plans and to picture the three-dimensional spaces they represent, in combination with visiting the site to experience the relationship of the structure to its surroundings or laying out a remodeling job inside your existing home, will give you a feel for the finished home and spare you much expense and annoyance.

Part II

Building Elements and Their Role in Shaping Life Experiences

5

Entrances

Whether they lead into the home or into each separate room, all entrances in your residence are responsible for creating a specific appropriate emotional setting for the space entered. Your spirit should be filled with pleasant anticipation when you see your home, with a sense of intimate recognition as you enter your property, and with contentment as you cross the threshold into your home. Likewise, the entrance to each individual room should help you make an appropriate transition to the experience of that room. If any of these feelings do not arise, the entrance needs mending.

The First Exterior Threshold of Your Home

Your home actually has three thresholds. The first is an exterior threshold. It occurs at the moment of instant recognition, when you round a corner or otherwise get close enough to get your first glimpse of your home. In that nanosecond, the breath of "I'm home" is released. Is this feeling positive or negative? What is seen from the most frequently traveled path to your home should make you smile, feel acknowledged, or feel empowered. Although the list is eclectic, here are some architectural choices to consider and some to avoid.

"How you approach a building—how you get into it and how you feel when you are there—has carried right through, as a main concern in my work."

PHILIP JOHNSON,
architect

EXPERIENCES AT THE FIRST THRESHOLD OF YOUR HOME

Potentially Positive	Potentially Negative
Window boxes	Utility area
Meandering path to entrance	Driveway
Window of main gathering room	Window of bathroom
Distinguishing trim or detail	Undistinguished wall
Mostly windows and a door	A garage that dominates the home's facade
Fences, hedge, gate, trellis, mailbox	Garbage cans, utility shed

---

The Second Exterior Threshold of Your Home

The second threshold starts when you physically cross the border to your own property. The moment that you take your first step onto your property or when your car's wheels hit the driveway is when the intimacy of home will begin to be felt. For townhouse, condominium, or apartment dwellers, the entry door is that second threshold. Like a kiss or a handshake, physical contact cements the somatic feel of home. A gate swinging effortlessly open or an even path underfoot makes contact amiable.

At this second threshold, the pathway to the door becomes visible. Having access to a footpath from all potential approaches is a feng shui essential. Figure 5.1a shows an entryway approach that has incorrect feng shui, while Figure 5.1b is one example of the multipath approach that is prescribed for entrances.

Figure 5.1 (a) Incorrect feng shui. A home's entrance pathway should reach all areas from which visitors may approach. Further, no vegetation should obscure the welcoming vista of a front door. (b) Correct feng shui. The entrance can be reached from the driveway and sidewalk or curb. While the door is clearly visible, the pathway to it slows you down and prepares you to feel relaxed upon reaching the threshold.

Here are a few suggestions for the second threshold that will enhance the joy of homecoming.

WHAT TO EXPERIENCE AT THE SECOND THRESHOLD

Potentially Positive	Potentially Negative
Supportive material underfoot	Slippery, bumpy, cracked, or uneven material underfoot
A well-oiled gate or door	A hard-to-open gate or door
An easy-to-negotiate path	A steep or hard-to-follow path
Wind chime or hanging plants	Unused hooks or empty places obviously meant to contain something
Sweet-smelling plants	Unkempt bed of plants
Quality door handle	Hard-to-operate door handle

The Third Threshold of Your Home

The third and last threshold is at the juncture of outside and inside. It is the transition of passing through the door. What is first seen and experienced weighs heavily on our first feelings of being home. How it is personalized sets a tone for how the occupants feel about themselves and their guests. Is there enough space around the threshold to accommodate a chair, table, or potted plant? What surfaces exist to encourage placing baskets for notes, nameplates, or artifacts that reveal the inhabitants' preferences? Decorative hooks or a niche ready to accept an object will encourage a family to personalize this last threshold of the home. Fresh flowers and natural or electric lighting to ease the transition to the darker interior are other suggestions for the passage into the interior space.

If you shudder to see a "we tried to drop off a package" slip slung around the handle of your front door, Figures 5.2 and 5.3 might be a solution. The drop-off bin located behind the shutters shown in Figure 5.3 hides an interior cabinet that is locked from inside. The cabinet inside can also be used as a shoe receptacle; a storage bin for umbrellas, snow gear, or seasonal necessities; or any other use deemed appropriate for the space. A small pane of glass on the inside doors can alert you to the arrival of a package.

Figure 5.2 The shutters to the right of the entrance door open onto a drop-off box for packages.

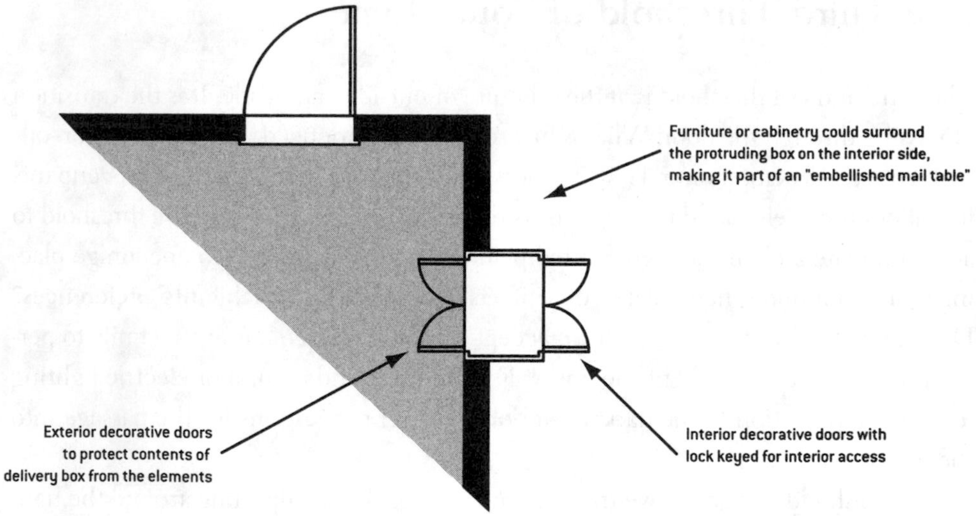

Figure 5.3 A detail of the drop-off box as it pierces the exterior wall into the interior space.

Furniture or cabinetry could surround the protruding box on the interior side, making it part of an "embellished mail table"

Exterior decorative doors to protect contents of delivery box from the elements

Interior decorative doors with lock keyed for interior access

For practical reasons, we don't always enter a home through the front door. If a secondary entrance like a door from a garage or other service area is the main family entrance, plan this threshold with the same care as the architectural main door. All well-traveled points of entry into the home must evoke positive expectations consistent with the spirit of home. Consider the options in Figure 5.4 when planning a home or remodeling your existing one.

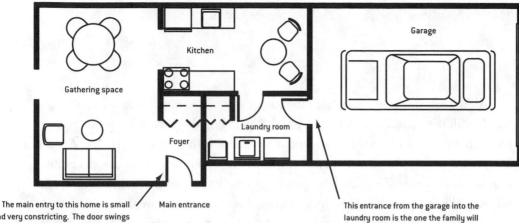

The main entry to this home is small and very constricting. The door swings in such a way as to block the view of the main living space and instead forces movement into a blank wall with a view of the closet straight ahead.

This entrance from the garage into the laundry room is the one the family will actually use most.

a.

The closets for the main entry and the laundry room could be reconfigured to give more space to the foyer. This creates an entry that is much more open, functional, and pleasing.

The entrance from the garage into the home was moved from the laundry room into the breakfast nook. The entry sequence becomes much more pleasant as occupants can be greeted first by a more social living space rather than a room dedicated to household chores.

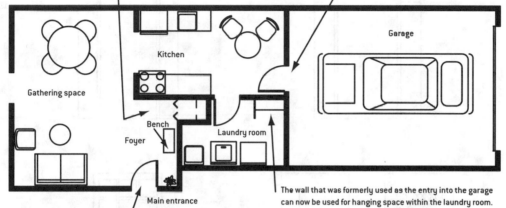

The wall that was formerly used as the entry into the garage can now be used for hanging space within the laundry room.

Changing the door swing allows for a much more gracious entry into the home. Circulation flows into the more open living space and allows the remaining solid wall to be used more efficiently. A small piece of furniture could be placed along the wall to provide a positive aesthetic focal point as well as a functional resting spot. This demonstrates compassion for those entering.

b.

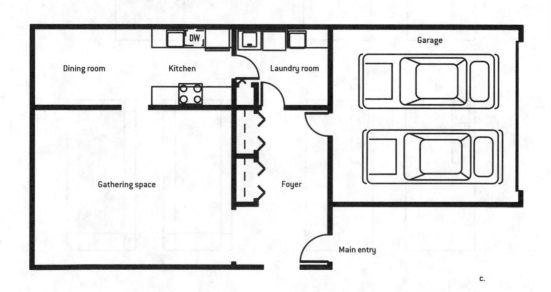

c.

Figure 5.4
(a) Having two doors leading inside, one from a garage, is the same as having a front and back door in a home, one being the utility entrance necessary when bringing groceries home and the other more nurturing with a foyer leading into the social areas. (b) A more gracious, welcoming first access to the home even from the garage is provided by entering a foyer that leads into the kitchen and toward the gathering spaces. (c) Best feng shui allows entry from both the front and garage doors to share a single, gracious foyer.

All too often the entrance from the garage leads its occupants into a service area that has all the appeal of a dirty dish towel. Upgrading the look of a door or even the trim around it can alter a utilitarian and less than nurturing garage entrance. Another suggestion, a rather minimal alteration within the scheme of building a structure, is to have two doors leading from the garage into the interior. A more ornate or upscale one would open up to the front foyer and another to a service area.

The choice of door reinforces the emotional feel of the entrance. Aside from aesthetic preference, be aware that a door's shape communicates specific sentiments. Consider the door shapes and their individual messages in Figure 5.5.

Figure 5.5 (a) The arched form over the door gives it a softer shape, signifying relaxed, easy movement. (b) The triangular peak over the door animates and sends out signals of actions and excitement. (c) Depending on the view inside and out, glass inserted in front doors can be either opaque or translucent. In both cases they will permit light to enter while it is your choice to select that which reveals or obscures the interior. (d) Adding small squares of either glass or raised materials diminishes any intimidation a large door might produce toward young people. (e) Details on one side of a door suggest that you are able to accept change and diversity and that you look to the future rather than dwell on the past. (f) Framing a door with trim or panels enhances its importance the same way a frame does a painting.

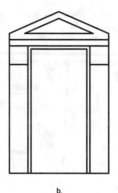

a.

b.

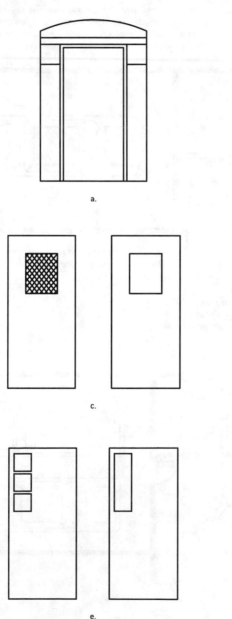

c.

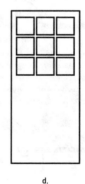

d.

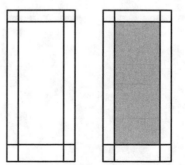

e.

f.

Inside the Home

Once inside the home, consider each room's threshold. It is important to align each entrance with an actual or visual reference appropriate to the space. Entrances to kitchens and dining rooms that transmit frenzy, for example, do not harmonize with the rooms' purposes.

Since every line and color has an emotional meaning, use only those that best promote the message of the room about to be entered. The following table is useful for selecting the color of a door leading into a home. Some colors are not directly associated with a line or shape, but mixing them with certain shapes or lines reinforces a message. See Chapter 9 for more information on the use of color.

THE EMOTIONAL MESSAGE OF DOOR COLOR AND SHAPE

Dominant Color	Message
Red	Energetic, attracts attention
Terra-cotta, browns, taupe	Security, stability, dependable
Silver, gold, copper, white	Discernment, focus, conservative
Blue	Emotionally present, self-involved
Green	Energetic, willing to be flexible, friendly

Dominant Color and Shape	Message
Pink, adobe, salmon with wavy curves	Relaxed, laid back, soothing
Turquoise with round shapes	Focused on higher mental processes, intellectual
Black with round shapes	Self-absorbed, intense, exotic, distant
Orange with squares	Centered around family life
Yellow with triangles	Strength, vigor, and clarity

Just as a book's cover can condense the essence of its contents, entrances are the distillation of what those entering will find inside your home. Personalization is perhaps the single most important feature in exterior entrances; appropriate space to accommodate a room's purpose is the most meaningful feature in planning interior entrances. Color and shape, in particular, convey a multitude of messages. Like first impressions, entrances carry a great deal of weight.

6

Gathering Spaces

Ideally the main gathering space serves as a home's heart. It nurtures all family members, both collectively and individually. In a sense it returns us to the mutually supportive lifestyle of our cave-dwelling ancestors, who would no more have separated various functions than nature would have come up with a life form that had two bodies, one for arms and the other for legs. The notion of separate rooms for independent activities evolved over time, and it's worth thinking about how several rooms constructed for separate activities might disrupt the synergy of a family unit. Especially today, with computers and other electronic media central to our daily functioning, our gathering spaces need to be flexible enough to encourage family members to come together, whether their goal is to socialize or pursue personal interests.

Figure 6.1 provides an alternative to a one-level gathering space and introduces the benefits of a plan that has several alternative spaces encircling the main gathering area. These spaces are defined by the vertical separation provided by the two levels. The conversation pit supports socializing or individual activities such as reading, while the raised perimeters support an alternative place to watch TV (a swivel TV cabinet allows it to be watched from both the lower and raised areas), work on the computer, or engage in other activities. All of these areas can be observed from the main work area in the kitchen. In addition, the steps offer an alternative surface for youngsters to play on. (How many of us used the stairs for Slinky or as a forum for dolls and trucks?)

"One of the things that one always hopes to find in architecture is mood, a sense of atmosphere."

EDWARD LARRABEE BARNES, *architect*

The Flexible Gathering Space for Groups and Individuals

Gathering spaces have always been intended to house both social and personal activities. The parlor of earlier times was meant for conversation and game playing but also

Figure 6.1 A conversation pit may be a benefit because the nearby other level could be the repository for a computer or other ancillary activity centers that reinforce group communication and shared time.

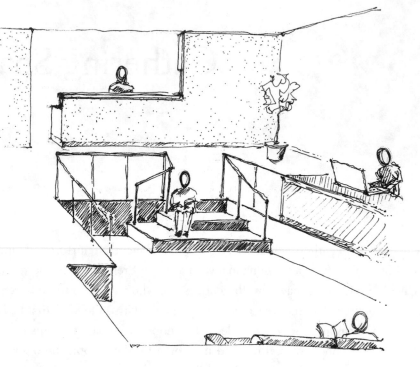

for reading. In the 1950s the typical furniture arrangement in gathering spaces changed forever to accommodate television watching, eliminating seating from the fourth wall to make room for the TV. But many families were uncomfortable with devoting their living room mainly to such passive, unsociable entertainment—or at least they were unwilling to sacrifice a wall and give up their idea of the aesthetically perfect living room furniture arrangement—and thus arose the den, family room, or great room of today. The den became the TV room, and the formal living room was reserved for entertaining guests. As we have discussed, however, a formal gathering space that is used infrequently is not only bad economics but also bad feng shui. We believe that your goal for the main gathering space in your home should be to accommodate as many group and individual activities as possible so the family will come together often—that is, your goal should be to ensure that your gathering space really functions as the heart of the home.

Different families, of course, have different needs. Yours may need more than one gathering space, especially if your family is large and diverse in its interests. But even if you allow for two or more gathering spaces, you would be wise to make sure that each one serves multiple functions so that each will indeed be a place to gather rather than a place to hole up separately. Articulating your overall goals for your home will help you uncover how many hearts or gathering spaces your home should have.

FUNCTIONS SERVED BY A GATHERING SPACE

For Individuals	For Groups
Homework	Conversation
Reading	Game playing
Game playing	Cooking
Television watching	Dining
Music listening	Music listening
Music playing	Music playing
Dining	Mending, cleaning, fixing
Telephone communication	Group meeting space
Computer use	Hobbies
Event planning	
Snoozing	
Entertaining	
Individual and group special interests such as yoga, meditation, exercise, and play	

Use this list as a jumping-off point. What other individual and group activities do your gathering spaces need to allow? Now think about where your family already pursues these activities. How many redundancies exist in your home? Do you really need these options, or do you find that a certain activity—say, TV watching or game playing—is always (or mostly) done in one particular room? Should you move what you need for a certain activity to a different room? For example, would a computer placed in a gathering space encourage family members to do things side by side?

There are many ways to create flexible private spaces in more public rooms. Building a window niche, a dormer, or a right-angled closet can provide the backdrop where private activities can flourish. Think small! A triangular ledge in a gathering space's corner that is just large enough for a laptop can encourage family members to gravitate to that room. (Other common areas of the house, while not strictly gathering spaces, become more communal when you give family members individual as well as collective ownership of them. Try reserving a kitchen surface for homework, installing a hallway bin to house toys, adding a bookshelf to a bathroom, or putting a surface at table height in a dormer. This way you can create flexible personal spaces throughout your home.) The ultimate in flexibility for gathering spaces is to make sure you have plenty of portable storage units, small tables, and trays on wheels to adapt the space to individual needs. Remember, almost all things stored can be put on wheels and moved as needed. Closet planners do it all the time!

Depending on your needs, a gathering room can always be set up to tip the scale toward personal activities or social activities. Figure 6.2 shows a few different ideas for providing space for individual or specialized activities within a gathering space, with varying emphases on the personal versus the social functions.

Computer stations are practically essential in a gathering space these days, especially if you want the children in the family to be present. One way to give a gather-

Figure 6.2 (a) A conversation pit allows the focus of a heart to be on communication while still allowing space for ancillary activities. (b) This floor plan shows a setup for a computer or musical niche as a companion to a gathering space.

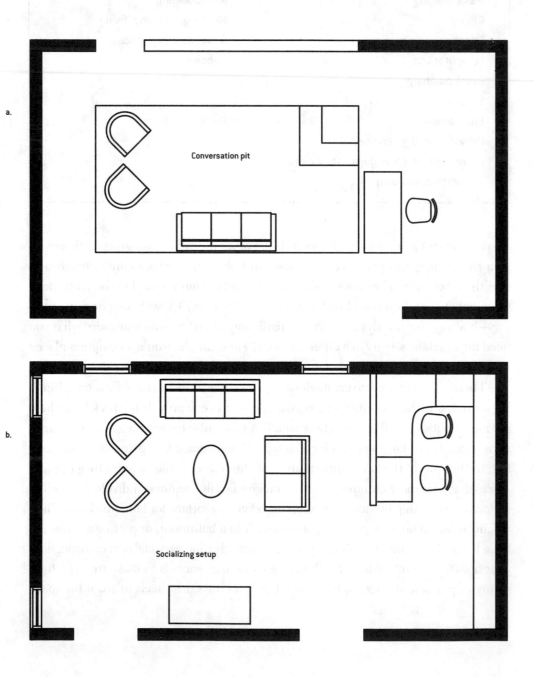

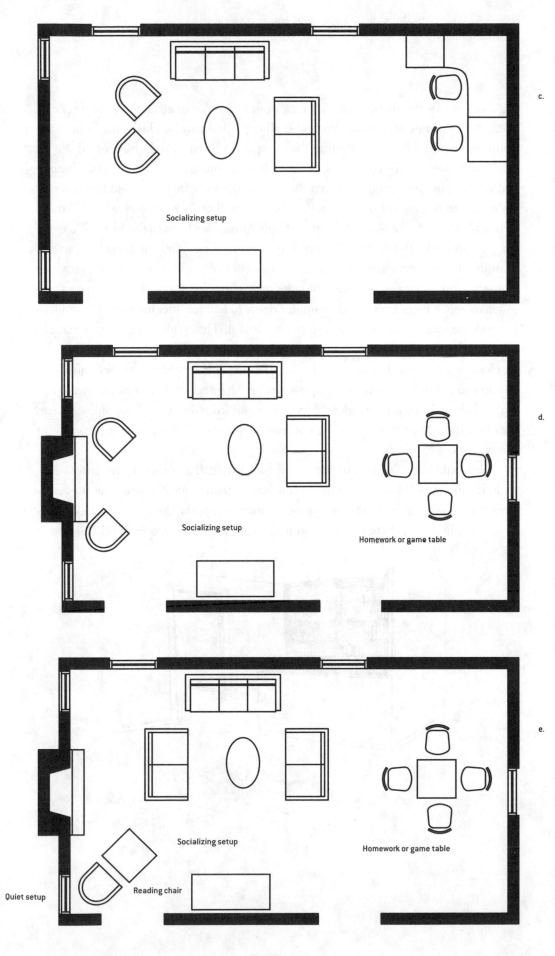

Socializing setup

Socializing setup

Homework or game table

Socializing setup

Homework or game table

Quiet setup **Reading chair**

c.

Figure 6.2 (c) We recommend that in homes with children, the computer monitor should face wall. It is our belief that the need for parents to monitor their children's Internet access exceeds the feng shui tenet to avoid sitting with your back to a room. (d) A table close to a seating setup provides flexible space for homework, games, or hobbies. (e) Having a space for conversation, a table for homework, games, or hobbies, and a solo reading chair affords the greatest flexibility in this gathering room.

d.

e.

ing space the necessary flexibility is to use built-in stations or attractive computer cabinets—even whole self-contained home offices—that can be closed up to hide the computer when not in use. Putting the computer station in a slightly set-off area is one way to provide for concentration as well as encourage connectedness. The person working on the computer screen should not, however, be positioned facing a wall unless there is a mirror or other reflective surface there, giving a view of the room behind him or her. Looking at a wall not only turns one's back to the heart of a space but also precludes the depth view necessary to prevent eye fatigue in the short run and maintain healthy eyes in the long run. The absence of alternating near and far views is one reason many people's eyesight deteriorates after hours spent looking at a computer screen. The person at the computer needs to have an incentive to look or focus beyond the screen, and architecture can provide it. That said, it is also important to consider the amount of glare a window will reflect on a computer's monitor should it be close to a window. In one space I used a fabric panel screening one section of the window to cut the glare on a desktop computer. Architecturally you can separate two windows by a wall wide enough to shield a monitor from the sun's glare. Sidewalls can also box the monitor in, ensuring complete protection from any sun beaming in through those windows.

We would like to make a strong case for what we call a home's *nerve center* being included in any building or remodeling job. Rather than sequester computer uses away from the hub of family activity, we suggest using a computer kiosk with doors, as illustrated in Figure 6.3 (here we envision it between a gathering room and the dining

Figure 6.3 This computer kiosk functions as a wall and divides one space into two. When in use, those inside will be integrated into the common spaces in a catbird seat between activity areas; when not in use, the kiosk makes an aesthetic contribution to both rooms.

area/kitchen), to position the nerve center near the heart of a home. For those now requiring silence to function at a computer, we believe that over time it is possible to screen out distracting sounds, as evidenced by most people's ability to screen out the television. Just as most of us have learned to render the sound of TV innocuous, it is possible to use the computer in the midst of family activity. Further, you might consider facing the computer monitor toward the room's entrance or most frequently used area to supervise the appropriateness of what your children view on the computer.

What activities function appropriately alongside a television? What activities can coexist with television's ubiquitous sounds? Would a computer with earphones be appropriate? Would an extra surface or table keep a hobbyist with the group without destroying his or her concentration? How can a room strike a balance between stimulating and relaxing, between promoting interaction and encouraging contemplation? If your goal is to nurture time spent with your family, the more inclusive a gathering space is, the better.

A Magnet to Attract Activity

Like our heart muscle, the heart of a home is a place for pulsating activity. The more central and diverse the gathering room is, the more likely a home will be lively and vibrate with the kind of verve that is the source of contentment. A gathering space is the focal point of family life and should draw the occupants to it like a fountain does in a plaza's center. For that reason, it is essential that your gathering space have a clearly defined feature as its magnet.

Traditionally, fireplaces and entertainment centers have acted as magnets drawing people into a space. They are, however, not the only possibilities. Consider how to integrate other embellishments that will draw people into the space. Your magnet could be as simple as lighting playing on a wall, spectacular pictures, a bird feeder outside a window to bring movement into a still space. It could be built-in shelving filled with artwork, games, books, or other much-loved items. In any case, be sure that all your gathering spaces motivate family members to use them.

Space for Socializing

There are a few considerations to remember to make rooms comfortable for social interaction. Keeping these ideas in mind will help you make a gathering space alluring. First, most seating should be seen and easily reached from the threshold of the room. A sofa positioned with its back to the entrance of a room is not conducive to socializing because the first impression of the room doesn't highlight a place to socialize.

Second, rooms for entertaining and comfortable interaction should have right-angle seating, which encourages intimate conversation. Right angles provide ease of communication based on a biological need for safety—humans are most comfortable when their vital organs are obscured or do not directly face another person.

It is best to have enough space to accommodate at least two right-angled seating arrangements when building a room to encourage interaction because humans feel more comfortable when we have options to choose from. Few of us like to feel forced to do anything; when there are less than two options for seating in a given space, we may subconsciously feel irked.

Spaces for Relaxing and Concentrating

When the area behind seating feels secure, the seated person can fully relax. Avoiding pathways behind the major seating area is one way to enhance a room's capacity for relaxation. Not all rooms need walls to define their perimeter, but in gathering spaces care must be given to the position of pathways, entrances, and vulnerable windows in relation to the major seating area.

The direction a window faces is therefore critical to the overall daytime experience of a space. Natural lighting is more yang (energizing) than yin (relaxing). Should a conversation area need to support calm rather than lively talk during the day, this space should be placed away from sun-filled windows.

The chart on page 127 will help you determine how the direction in which the windows face will affect your gathering spaces. Note that this chart is for the Northern Hemisphere only. Change as necessary for the Southern Hemisphere.

Spaces for Energizing and Invigorating

Light is the architectural equivalent of a pep pill. A type of depression known as *seasonal affective disorder (SAD)* is linked directly to light deprivation. In her book *The Power of Place: How Our Surroundings Shape Our Thoughts, Emotions, and Actions,* Winifred Gallagher tells us that native Alaskans suffer less from SAD-type winter depressions than people who have moved north from the lower forty-nine states. This

THE PROS AND CONS OF DIFFERENT WINDOW EXPOSURES

Direction	Time of Day	Benefits	Potential Disadvantage
North	All day	Relaxed atmosphere at all times	Doesn't promote high energy
South	Mornings	Evokes optimism	May be an irritant for those who wake up slowly
South	Afternoons	Lingering daylight draws use	Can distract from concentrating
East	Mornings	Energizes and activates	Can promote self-involvement
East	Afternoons	Appropriate for winding down	If inside all day can be disheartening
West	Mornings	Allows for a slow entry into the day's routine	Does not add enthusiasm for beginning a day
West	Afternoons	Can be a mesmerizing focus	Can distract interactions

is true in part, she explains, because traditional Alaskan culture encourages outdoor activities during daylight hours, however brief, while people who adhere to the traditional business schedule remain inside and are denied the benefit of the day's sunlight. Good lighting planning is key to activating spaces. During evening hours, intense lighting sources over seated areas will help compensate for days spent indoors.

Because the eye seeks light (and, hence, energy), skylights, as shown in Figure 6.4, can be used as space enhancers. A hallway can be adorned with a skylight. A piece

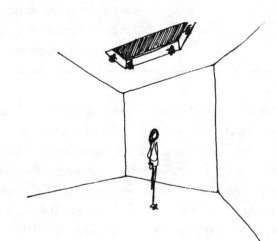

Figure 6.4 Skylights punctuate dark areas, casting light in areas that do not typically have natural lighting—transition areas, pathways, work areas—or simply flooding spaces not enhanced by light from a window. By framing a skylight with electric light, you retain the benefit at night.

of furniture can be highlighted with a skylight, as can a room's path of movement. Framing a skylight with electric lights ensures that its benefits will be consistent, regardless of the natural lighting conditions. Skylights allow the most direct light in and can, if properly positioned, ensure the brightest amount of light during the day. This in turn bestows the most energy-producing natural feature into a space.

Planning Gathering Spaces for Diverse and Changing Needs

Finally, consider a gathering space a womb that provides everything a family needs for growth and development. If life is a process with change as its central characteristic, spaces that can adapt as needs evolve are optimal. Children get older, your own interests shift, and physical changes alter the way you interact with space. All these factors must be considered in shaping the way a space is experienced by mixed age and gender groups. Consider the following list when planning spaces so that they will function easily over time.

CONSIDERATIONS FOR CREATING A FLEXIBLE SPACE

Item	Consideration
Light switches	Height for young or wheelchair bound
Electronic equipment	Access for safety and convenience
Window manipulation	Safety and degree of difficulty to open
Shelves	Adjustability
Doors	Weight and swing
Latches or knobs	Ease of use or unobstruction
Electrical outlets	Position for convenience and likely location of equipment

---

In a world increasingly characterized by isolating activities, longer periods away from home, and mobility, it is architecture's task to nourish and support a strong nucleus with design that fulfills the basic human requirement for kinship and belonging. Humans are not meant to live in isolation—we are group oriented. With contemporary lifestyles flinging families to the four corners of the country, if not the world, it is even more important for us to strengthen opportunities for socializing and connecting with others. Our homes' gathering spaces can fulfill this need if we attend to the features that enhance our desire to use these rooms.

7

Personal Spaces

Bedrooms, Studies, and Home Offices

Every home needs spaces for the use of one individual rather than for communal activity. While these personal spaces may be shared, they have to serve the idiosyncratic needs of the individuals who use them. These spaces range from bedrooms to studies and home offices or niches designed for similar purposes. Because these areas typically serve limited functions, they can be constructed with a specificity that few gathering spaces allow. For example, task lighting around a couple's bed must accommodate each person's height. The first decision is where to locate the personal spaces in the context of the entire house and in relation to the exterior.

Positioning Bedrooms

My childhood bedroom was directly across from the top of the stairs. My sister's bedroom was down the hall, adjacent to our parents' room. Since my bedroom was buffered from our parents by closets and a bathroom, I essentially had a wing of my own, perfect for a child like me, who craved independence. My sister, on the other hand, coveted our parents' attention, and so her bedroom's location was ideal for her. Consider each inhabitant's preferences when choosing locations.

Even when the options for locating bedrooms are not ideal, there are ways to compensate. As shown in Figure 7.1, private space may be buffered from other rooms with closets, bathrooms, or other storage facilities. Dead air space muffles sound, and for those who need silence and remoteness these buffers can provide exactly the same benefits in an existing house as a brand-new layout.

Bedrooms positioned in front of or next to stairwells or terraces encourage independent thinking and even rebellious behavior. I probably never would have slipped silently out of the house as a teenager had it not been for the low-pitched roof outside

"A house is not an expression about society or technology; it's an expression of the people who live in it."

SARAH SUSANKA,
architect

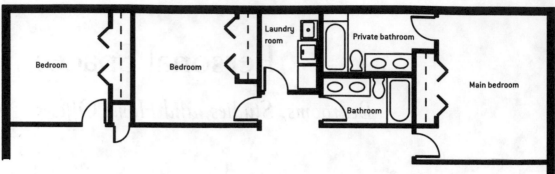

Figure 7.1 To ensure a bedroom's privacy, plan closets, laundry, and bathrooms to separate it from the others.

my bedroom window. This setup protected me from parental surveillance and set the stage for many misadventures after my parents had safely retired to their bedroom. On the positive side, an adolescent who needs encouragement to become more adventurous can benefit from the lure of independence that a room close to an exit route fosters.

A family with young children, however, usually will be best served if just the parents' bedroom is near the exits, as shown in Figure 7.2. No matter what style your home is, consider positioning the parents' bedroom in the guardian position, much as a sentry box would protect the treasures of a castle.

In general it is best for bedrooms not to be positioned near the family's most frequently used entrance. The rooms we encounter first when entering a home are perceived as most important, so common rooms are therefore better positioned near entrances.

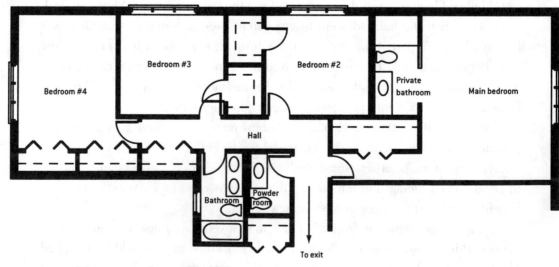

Figure 7.2 A parents' bedroom is best positioned nearest the exits, in feng shui termed the *guardian position.*

On a recent trip to Italy, I was invited to see the renovation of an ancient stone house by a well-known architect. The imposing front entrance led me into a spacious foyer ample enough for a grand round table standing in the center. Three bedrooms opened onto this entrance foyer. A narrow staircase that descended to one side was the sole pathway leading to the gathering spaces and master bedroom. Even though this home was only a weekend retreat for a family with grown children, I imagined that this layout of private spaces close to the main entrance would do little to contribute to this home's appropriate functioning. The house was meant as a hideaway for relaxation, but the layout encouraged the family members to remain isolated from one another.

Personal Spaces Within Bedrooms

Many people find it helpful to have a quiet place for paperwork, recreational reading, or just relaxing away from the hue and cry of the rest of the house. Often the best location for these retreats is within an existing bedroom, because the bedrooms are usually already removed from the gathering spaces. Although assigning two functions to a bedroom poses some challenges, it can be an economical solution when there is no possibility of using a whole extra room without building an addition.

PERSONAL AREAS TO CONSIDER WITHIN BEDROOMS

Adult's Bedroom Areas	Children's Bedroom Areas
Bill paying	Studying
Letter writing	Drawing
Dressing and grooming	Dressing and grooming
Using telephone	Using telephone
Relaxing, reading	Relaxing, reading
Watching TV or videos	Playing with electronic hand-held games
	Spending time with friends

From childhood on, desks often find their way into children's rooms, perhaps not as an integral architectural feature but simply as a repository for objects used in small motor-skill activities, which often accumulate as clutter. Using closets to form desk cubicles or niches and to define circulation paths as shown in Figure 7.3 follows the feng shui principle of keeping work areas visually separate from rest areas.

Figure 7.3
(a) Closets make natural side walls for study niches in a bedroom. (b) Positioning a closet away from an exterior wall permits a study niche.

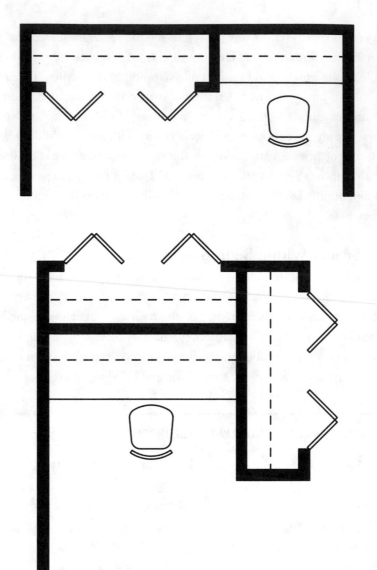

However, if space is not available, raising a sleeping platform over a desk area, as shown in Figure 7.4, or using a bowed window for a desk niche as in Figure 7.5 can help separate functions in a bedroom.

Figure 7. 6 shows another way that work or more public space can be separated from more private space, in this case in the parents' master suite. The sitting/dressing/storage room is the first part of the suite that is seen from the entrance. Its position and the closets that flank the entrance to the master bedroom preserve the sleeping space as a true personal/private retreat.

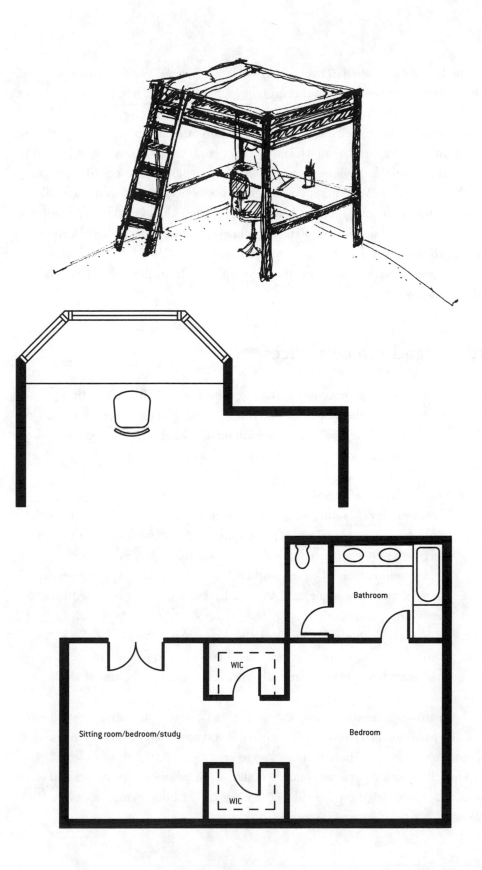

Figure 7.4 Sleeping lofts create a yin-type atmosphere for study niches.

Figure 7.5 Window recesses permit a cozy study niche, especially in small rooms.

Figure 7.6 Planning a bedroom sitting/dressing space before reaching the bedroom buffers the sleeping zone and provides a meeting space for other family members.

Bathroom

WIC

Sitting room/bedroom/study

Bedroom

WIC

Finally, consider whether two people will be sharing any of the bedrooms in your home. Sharing the space doesn't mean that each individual's needs cannot be met. How many of us sharing bedrooms have denied ourselves the opportunity to read in the middle of the night because light would disturb our partner? Ordinary bed table lamps won't let one person read while the other person sleeps. However, task lighting, contained and shielded from extended illumination, can be the key to managing a shared private space. Whether a down light is positioned exactly over the reader in bed or over a chair, task lighting is essential for individual comfort. Grooming is another issue of the shared bedroom. Not all people feel comfortable performing all of their grooming needs in front of a partner. Creating a shield, be it a wall, folding screen, or row of plants, separating the grooming area from the sight line of the bed or sitting area makes sense.

Studies and Home Offices

The epitome of personal space in a home might be a home office. Everything can be tailored to the needs of the individual who will be working in the space. Here are some questions to consider before selecting the location of studies and other personal places or areas that require concentration. Answer yes or no.

Test for Location of Studies
1. I find sounds distracting when I want to concentrate or simply be by myself.
2. I dislike feeling isolated and separated from others and find the sound of their voices or activities comforting even when focused on a project.
3. I am happiest alone when my world is tranquil and devoid of distractions.
4. I love an animated scene, and seeing a backyard or street filled with people is reassuring to me.
5. If I had my druthers, I would lock the door when I want to be alone.
6. Even when working or relaxing alone, I don't like to feel out of the loop and often react to or get involved with what is going on in the rest of my home.

If you answered mostly yes to questions 1,.3, and 5, your home office or study space should be positioned far from activity centers. If you answered mostly yes to questions 2, 4, and 6, your private space can be close to activity centers.

The following are just a few fundamental feng shui principles for studies and home offices. For more detail on this subject, see my earlier book *Feng Shui Goes to the Office*.

Feng Shui Suggestions for Home Offices

- Treat the office door as a front door and place an identifying icon on the outside.
- Position a desk so that it faces the door or have a mirrored object reflect the door so you can see it.
- Have intermittent sound from a ticking clock or a bell looped over a file or desk drawer.
- Install some object that produces movement such as an outside bird feeder, a mobile near an air vent, or a clock with a pendulum.
- Diffuse at least one scent into the atmosphere each day.
- Have enough storage space hidden from view.
- Have the telephone jack accessible to the ear you most likely listen from.
- Position a desk's task lighting over the nondominant hand.

As discussed in Chapter 6, you may want to consider creating a nerve center, which has a sense of separateness but is still within the sight line to the heart of the home. One possibility is to carve out a space for the nerve center in a less utilized room such as the dining room or formal living room. This proximity would allow easy access to the computer for the entire family.

If our private spaces are designed appropriately, we can better cultivate what we wish for ourselves. Feng shui's wisdom suggests that we are as successful as the spaces we create for ourselves to succeed in. The trick is balance. Just as a long row of cubicles does nothing to promote cohesiveness in business, a home without well thought out personal spaces can separate its members from the home's emotional vortex. Yet a home without spatial opportunities for members to be by themselves outside of the scrutiny of other family members is just as potentially damaging. The proper distribution of personal spaces brings balance.

Bathrooms, Dressing Spaces, and Closets

8

The care we give our bodies mirrors the intrinsic regard we have for ourselves. Yet in contemporary Western culture far too much emphasis is placed on shaping our image rather than on rejoicing in what is. Many of us focus on our perceived deficits or inadequacies in our personal care. Remodeling, adding on, or building a new home gives you the opportunity to dispel such negativity by creating grooming spaces that really soothe and invigorate you rather than polish up your image.

The ideas in this chapter range from the simplest remodeling measures, like removing the mirror from your bathroom vanity, to building whole new closets or bathrooms. Most of our notions of what a bathroom, a closet, or a dressing room should look like come from manufacturers of fixtures or designers of high-end model homes. The bathrooms are walled with mirrors, the closets fitted out with intricate configurations of shelves and compartments. These are not necessarily what suits us individually, nor are they always what serves our spirit. We ask you to consider your private grooming areas with an open mind and a fresh eye to what works for you personally, not what looks good in a shelter magazine.

Where is it written that it is necessary to look in a mirror while brushing your teeth? Why should we be greeted at the front entrance by a mirror rather than a supportive, aesthetic piece of art? Why should a huge walk-in closet be filled from floor to ceiling with storage compartments when you might love instead to have a private space for dressing? The possibilities for these spaces should be limited only by what's right for you and your family. That includes, of course, practicality and convenience. If you have to bend across a sink to apply makeup or shave, if retrieving clothing is a juggling act, or if every time you turn around you meet your image in a mirror, these spaces for taking the best care possible of yourself may instead only add to your stress.

Yet these grooming spaces should have the opposite effect. If you have ever sunk into a soft recliner to have a facial, you know the luxury of the implied promise of beauty. Who has not felt like royalty when luxuriating in a hot tub of bubbles? Part of

"We must provide— through order—a background of serenity for today's feverish activity, and scale architecture to frame man happily in his environment."

MINORU YAMASAKI, *architect*

a spa's benefit is the way it envelops us in an environment of lush pampering. There are always hooks handy for our street clothes, cozy slippers to pad around in, sprays to hydrate the face, and creams to soften the skin. The dim, rosy lighting, the air laden with fragrance, and the peaceful, soothing sounds add to the ambience. No wonder we feel beautiful immersed in an environment that nurtures all of our senses. Props that support self-care bolster the way we think and feel about ourselves. The following ideas can be applied throughout your home to echo the feeling that you want from your grooming spaces.

Ambience That Makes Us Feel Beautiful

- Low-level lighting with intense lighting only over task areas
- Colors that enhance skin tones: red, rose, incandescent warm light sources (not fluorescent)
- Aromatics identified with tranquillity, such as lavender, rose, or jasmine, dispensed into the air
- Muffled machine sounds that replicate nature's sounds of water, bells, or clocks with gongs
- Mirrors only when appropriate for tasks (putting on makeup, checking your finished look after dressing)
- Mirrors lit with low-level, golden-toned lighting (incandescent)

Bathrooms

An architect and feng shui practitioner recently told me that during the "growing years" of his four teenagers, three of whom were girls, their sinks and vanities were located in the hall; the toilet was in a separate "water closet." Seldom did the typical "who's using the bathroom and for how long" conflict arise, and the mornings were often marked by conversation as the family members brushed their teeth together. Mirrors for makeup were relegated to bedrooms.

This kind of change may or may not be possible for you. Placement of sinks, toilets, showers, and bathtubs is often determined by the location of plumbing pipes. For that reason we are not necessarily going to recommend a total overhaul; plumbing swells building costs considerably.

What is important to consider first when building or remodeling is whether there is an appropriate buffer between public spaces like kitchens, gathering areas, and dining areas and the adjacent bathrooms. You should not be able to see the interior of a bathroom from a common area when the bathroom door is open, or to see a person entering the bathroom. The least expensive remedy is to rearrange the furniture in the gathering room to avoid a view of the bathroom. If this is impractical for you, the problem can be mitigated by rehanging the bathroom door to open in the opposite direction.

When considering buffers between a bathroom and common areas, consider scents and sounds as well as visibility. The most awkward master bedroom/bathroom/dressing area configuration I ever saw was in an upscale gated community near my home. Within its master suite, with its volume ceiling, the standard eight-foot bathroom wall stopped several feet short of the ceiling! The builder had not shown the slightest regard for how odors from the bathroom would affect the occupants in the adjacent bedroom. No doubt this was a cost-saving measure, but the enforced sharing of experiences could hardly have been a romance builder. A wall or scent barrier definitely should have met the ceiling.

As to bathrooms near the gathering areas of the house, closets, pantries, washer and dryers, and other utilitarian objects and spaces can be placed between the bathroom and the common areas, as shown in Figure 8.1, to give those using the bathroom reassuring distance. Also, consider cordoning off a water closet to separate the toilet (and bidet) from less private grooming activities.

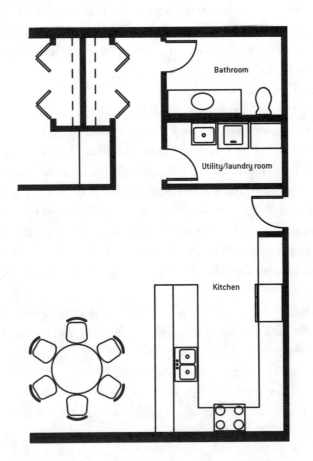

Figure 8.1 Bathrooms require privacy, and utility areas, closets, and infrequently used stairwells and passageways can provide excellent auditory and visual buffers.

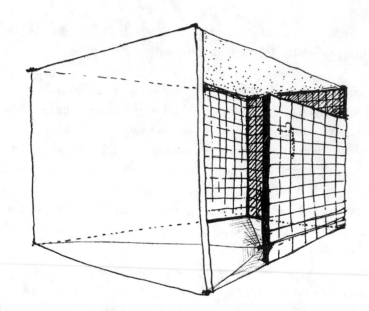

Finally, a word about life changes. Shower stalls can be constructed without a lip or raised threshold to accommodate wheelchairs. Figure 8.2 shows a fairly standard shower with an opening wide enough for a wheelchair, which also has a measure of privacy. Having such a bathing area makes sense, especially when it is adjacent to a ground-floor bedroom or other room that could be converted to a bedroom.

Mirrors and Their Effect

Traditional feng shui teachings have much to say about mirrors. One concept is that we should never see ourselves in a mirror upon awakening. The Chinese explanation is that the soul is not yet back in the body and harm could befall it. Our explanation, based more on Western psychology, is that waking is a transition, and at times of transition we are all inclined to be vulnerable since our defenses are not at the ready. Besides, few of us look our best when waking up, and our ego is bound to be bruised when the first image we have of ourselves each day is of messy hair and an awkward gait. Greeting our mirror reflection at this time of day rarely adds to a positive attitude. Therefore, mirrors should be located strategically in areas where it is imperative to see our image.

Following this reasoning, it is not necessary to have a mirror over the bathroom sink, between the sinks, or framing a sink. A grooming mirror can be placed on an accordion arm next to a sink, atop a dressing table, or on the back of a closet door. A window over a sink could serve you better in the morning, for a view to the outside may be more likely to inspire, delight, or energize you, as shown in Figure 8.3. A mirror can also be placed on the side of a sundry tower, as illustrated in Figure 8.4.

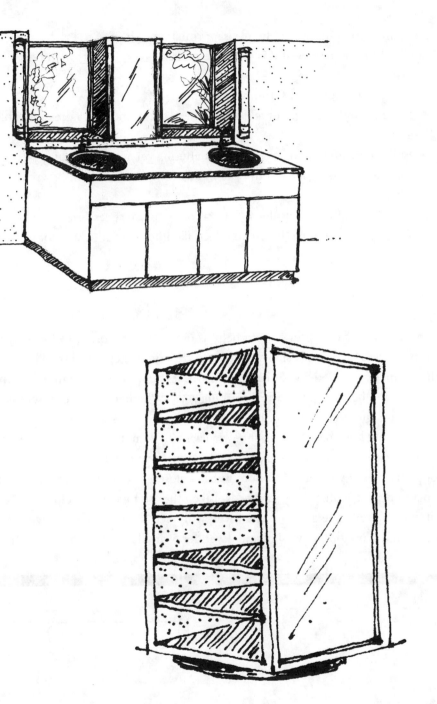

Figure 8.3 A window instead of a mirror over a bathroom sink may lead you away from self-criticism often doled out while examining your own image in a mirror.

Figure 8.4 A cube that swivels with a mirror on the back-side offers both storage capacity and grooming aids.

Dressing Spaces

Whether it is an alcove in a bedroom or bathroom or just a well-placed table, we all benefit from some kind of space to gather apparel, accessories, and grooming items.

Dressing and grooming should be pleasant rituals, and having the right space is just as beneficial to this activity as it is to all the others you participate in at home.

Ideas for Dressing and Grooming Areas

- Raise a window height or add a skylight to accommodate a dressing table and chair.
- Full-spectrum lighting can provide flattering yet accurate light.
- Include a dressing area in front of or adjacent to a closet, as shown in Figure 8.5.
- Install a shelf that folds down from a wall to place accessories on when dressing or grooming. It can be folded flat into the wall when not needed.

Closets

An entire industry has sprung up to help us organize our closets. In Chapter 10 we offer some ideas for closet design. Suffice it to say here that closets should be designed with specificity in mind. Whether you are five feet tall or six feet tall will definitely determine the best height for your clothing rods. Whether your feet resemble Cinderella's or Bigfoot's will certainly dictate how many shoes you can fit into a given space—but not how many pairs of shoes you actually own. For this reason, we strongly recommend that when you are planning closet space you make a list directly on your floor plan of what you intend to store in each closet. In that way you will see if you are planning adequately for your needs. Like other storage areas, closets should be positioned close to the areas in which you will need their contents. Having a linen closet near a ground-floor washer and dryer, for example, makes no sense if the bed-

Figure 8.5 A separate door in a long closet can create a dressing niche.

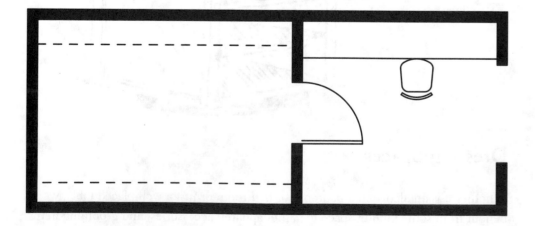

rooms and bathrooms are upstairs. Athletic equipment that's used often probably shouldn't be stored in the basement if the basement is not on the route to the exit family members will take to get to the tennis courts, golf club, ski slope, or ball field.

Consider the allocation of adequate space for the following closets when planning a new home, or adding one when remodeling.

Possible Storage Needs for Closets
- Hanging garments
- Shelves for linens, games, or foodstuffs
- Collections of albums, CDs, wines, cigars, videos
- Hobby needs, tools, sewing materials
- Seasonal items

The way we care for our bodies in many ways mirrors how we nurture ourselves on other levels. Taking time to sort out the intricacies of your personal needs indicates a willingness to care for other important areas of life. Health is not just a pill or the absence of illness; it is a condition resulting from daily administrations, and self-care is the first step. Make sure that the spaces you use for dressing, grooming, and self-care fulfill your needs.

Light Up and Color My World

Our daily rhythms are connected to the rising and setting of the sun. It is natural to awaken with the day's first light and wind down as the sun descends below the horizon. Like the sun, our energy is highest at midday. Sunlight releases hormones that promote optimism, whereas darkness disengages us from life. We have good reason to be concerned, then, about the legions of computer workers who work in rooms lit mainly by the glow of their computer screens. Living in perpetual dusk hardly promotes natural optimism or keeps hormonal systems in balance.

Natural light, with all its beneficial characteristics, supports our inborn rhythms throughout the day. Therefore it is a critical element in the design of every room in a house. Whether you are building from scratch, remodeling, or adding on to an existing home, you can use natural and artificial light not only to shape the overall experience of a room but also to create different effects in different parts of the space. When planning lighting, you need to consider the amount of light, the variation of intensity and pattern the light will cast, the placement of the sources of light, and the quality of the light. These three factors combined make for an infinite number of choices—with end results to suit every individual homeowner.

"Light is the medicine of the future."

JACOB LIBERMAN,
author

Natural Lighting

In Chapter 6 we listed the pros and cons of different window exposures at different times of day. The type of natural light that enters a room definitely has emotional effects on the people in the room and what they do there. Therefore, you should be sure to consider the time of day a room will be used before deciding which direction it should face. This advice, of course, applies mainly to those who are designing an entire home from scratch. If you are remodeling, you may have fewer choices, depending on how many outside walls each room will have and how much you can reallocate existing space.

If your morning routine centers primarily around dressing and grooming, it might be a good idea to put your bedroom and dressing area in a place where it will face east. If your family is in the habit of having dinner in the early evening, facing north, not west, may prevent strain caused by the angle of the setting sun. To make each room light-appropriate, you must pay close attention to the time frame within which a room is occupied.

As a rule, plan on positioning rooms used primarily in the morning so that they are filled with light from the east or the south, whereas rooms occupied primarily after two in the afternoon should face south or west. West light is suitable for gathering rooms, however, only as long as the sun does not interfere with or create a glare on seating areas during the room's use. North, the only direction without direct sunlight in the Northern Hemisphere, is a good place for rooms that are used for activities that require concentration. Within the context of your daily habits, consider these directions for the following rooms.

SUGGESTED DIRECTION FOR INDIVIDUAL ROOMS

Direction	Rooms
East	Breakfast room
Southeast	Porch, computer space, "away" room
Northeast	Bedroom
West	Evening gathering room
Southwest	Kitchen, dining room
Northwest	Library, playroom
North	Bathroom, storage, art or hobby space
South	Kitchen, gathering room, children's bedroom

Keep in mind, however, that other feng shui considerations might override these rules of thumb regarding direction. If, for example, putting a bedroom where it would face east would mean placing it near an entrance, it would be better to give the room a different exposure than to make the occupants feel uneasy, as being near an entrance would do.

Natural light comes not just from windows and doors but also from skylights. See Chapter 6 for information on use of skylights.

Electric Lighting

Artificial light is rarely sufficient by itself, but it is essential to replace natural light at night and sometimes to augment it during the day. Electric lighting can be installed on walls, on ceilings, or atop furniture. Before you plan the lighting for a room, consider the cone of light that will be thrown and make sure that you will have the right quantity and quality of light for the activities that will take place in the room. Figure 9.1 illustrates where light from different sources will be cast.

When you're planning lighting during building and remodeling design, also consider where you'll need outlets. Although the minimum number of electric outlets and the distance between them are mandated by building codes, you owe it to yourself to think purposely about the kind of lamps that will best suit your needs. Where is it written that all electric outlets have to be near the baseboard? If you have decided to place a credenza or table in a certain area, why not eliminate the long cord hanging down and raise the electrical outlet?

You may want to review the information on yin and yang in Chapter 1 to reinforce your knowledge about the differences between low-level and spot lighting (yin) and overall bright lighting (yang). Generally, rooms requiring concentration, rest or sleep, and individual activity should have yin lighting, while rooms for group activity and conversation should have yang lighting.

BENEFITS OF DIFFERENT TYPES OF LIGHTING

Type of Light	Benefits
Ceiling Lighting	
Whole-ceiling glow lighting	Obvious, without subtlety
Recessed spotlights	Good for lighting pathways
Eyeball spots	Can wash wall artwork with drama
Pin-light spots	Can highlight small objects
Track lighting	Can variegate an area with shadows and light
Decorative lighting	Creates a focus on light source as well as what it illuminates
Wall Lighting	
Single sconce	Adds texture and dimension in a space
Down lights with arm extensions	Focuses on task at hand
Lights that simulate candlelight	Romantic and mysterious
Neon art lighting	Adds drama in a space

Figure 9.1 (a) When the source of a bulb is flush with the ceiling such as with recessed can lighting, the illumination creates a general wash of light. This kind of light source is called *direct lighting* and provides general illumination with few fluctuations of intensity. Adds a crisp overall lighting.

(b) When a light source permits its illumination to radiate through an opaque surface (usually white glass), the light is called *general diffuse*. Throws off generally an even light that covers a nearby area. To softly highlight a wall or furniture below, use general diffuse lighting.

(c) When illumination is aimed only in one direction, in this case downward, the surfaces below are highlighted. Artwork, dining tables, and work areas can benefit from *semidirect* or *direct-indirect (upward) lighting*.

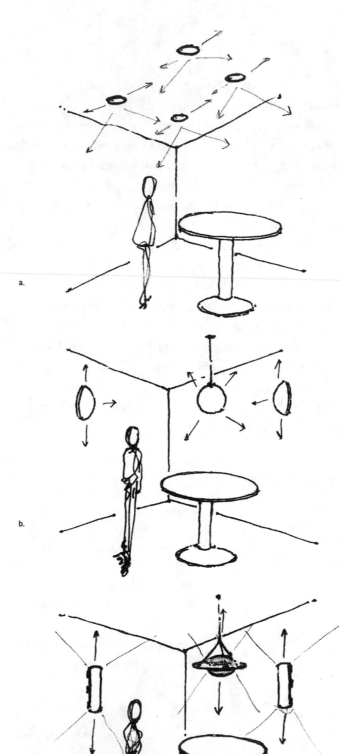

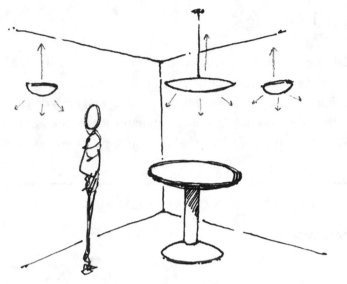

(d) *Semi-indirect lighting* aims most of the light upward on the ceiling with some downward or outwardly directed light.

d.

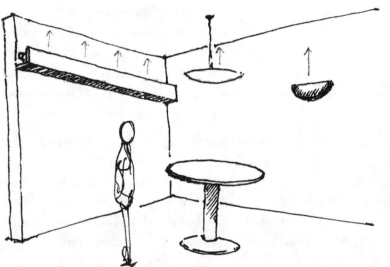

(e) *Up lighting* adds drama to a setting, for while it produces general illumination the use area remains mysteriously in shadow. Formal entrance foyers, guest bathrooms, and some passageways can be made more enticing with this indirect light that illuminates with low contrast and fewer shadows.

e.

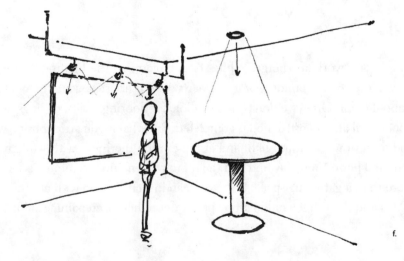

(f) Spotlights intensely illuminate and showcase what they are aimed toward. Used to focus attention on a painting, sculpture niches, or wall artifacts, they should be employed sparingly, or their impact will be diluted.

f.

Outdoor Lighting

Outdoor lighting is both utilitarian and dramatic. A spotlighted tree against a curtain of darkness can be enchanting, just as a row of lanterns following a pathway's edge is often charming. Lighting defies nighttime darkness and adds drama to a landscape. What is spotlighted and what is left dark communicates a story. Consider the following and decide for yourself if what is lit feels appropriate to who you are.

WHAT SPOTLIGHTING OUTDOOR AREAS COMMUNICATES

Illuminated Area	Communicates
Pathways	Friendliness; encourages contact
Front door	Desire to be noticed
Facade of home	Lack of fear of being known
Trees	Conscious of nature and trustworthy
Lawn	Need for order and control
Perimeter	Preference for emotional distance

Lighting both outside and inside can shape a room, underscore a message, or motivate and is integral to a structure's functioning. The architect Frank Lloyd Wright used the light patterns created by skylights and windows in his interiors as architectural statements. He consciously considered how light would interplay with interior surfaces and used it like a brushstroke of surface detail. Lighting should never be considered casually but exploited to underscore your home's personality.

Color

Light and color work in synergy. While you are planning the lighting for each room in a new home you are building or in the parts of your house you are remodeling, also think about color. Often we don't choose colors for flooring, walls, ceilings, windows, and doors until after construction is completed. But what if you are choosing windows to flood a room with natural light and also picturing the room with white walls and light-colored floors? You may find that the room will end up resembling a snow white-out more than a gathering space. Sure, you can in that case go with a softer color for your walls and floor. But wouldn't it be better not to have to repaint? And if you have a better idea up front of what you will like, you can make painting much easier by painting the contrasting trim before it's hammered into place.

To help you envision the results you'll get with different colors, be aware of the amount of light that each color reflects or absorbs. The more reflection a color has, the more attention it will garner. Remember, the eye naturally seeks the lightest surface. Contrasting surfaces are more easily noticed than ones that are adjacent to other ones that reflect light similarly. The overall brightness of a room created by window and artificial light can be enhanced or diminished by color. Reflect upon your choices and be sure they are appropriate for your desires.

AMOUNT OF LIGHT REFLECTED BY DIFFERENT COLORS AND MATERIALS

Material	Percentage of Light Reflected
White paint	75–85
Yellow paint	61–85
Light green paint	48–75
Light blue paint	34–61
Dark green paint or dark wood	11–25
Red bricks or medium red/brown walls	5–25
Natural concrete	5–50
Oak	40
Light fabrics	30–40
Beige wallpaper	56–72

Where Color Is Seen

Colors change depending on the angle from which they're viewed and where the colors are placed, as indicated in the two charts on page 152.

Meaning of Colors

In feng shui, five colors are associated with the elements:

- Black or dark blue is associated with water.
- Green is associated with wood.
- Red and red-orange are associated with fire.
- White and metallic colors are associated with metal.
- Yellow, brown, and terra cottas are associated with earth.

EFFECT OF COLORS SEEN FROM DIFFERENT ANGLES

Type of Color	Seen from Below	Seen from the Side	Seen from Above
Warm and light (sun-yellow, salmon)	Uplifting	Warming, activating, coming closer	Mentally stimulating
Warm and dark (red, brown, olive)	Feeling good, solid, earthy	Strong, enclosing	Locked, solemn, heavy
Cold and light (light blue, aqua, lavender)	Smooth, stimulating	Cool, leading away, expanding	Lighten, lifting
Cold and dark (dark green and blue)	Heavy, pulling down	Cold and feeling sad	Threatening, darkening

Source: International Institute for Bau-Biologie and Ecology

EFFECT OF COLORS WHEN USED ON DIFFERENT SURFACES

Color	Effect on Floors	Effect on Walls	Effect on Ceilings
Red	Impressive	Close, loud	Disturbing
Orange	Stimulating	Warm	Degrading
Yellow	Uplifting, hasty	Exciting	Stimulating
Green	Holding softly	Enclosing	Protecting
Blue	Lifting	Distant	Mentally uplifting
Brown	Earthy	Rigid	Pressing
Ochre	Sandy	Animating	Covering
Violet	Disturbing	Depressing	Depressing
Black	Deepening	Reversing	Weighing
Pink	Untouchable	Delicate	Diaphanous
White	Strange to touch	Neutral	Empty

Source: International Institute for Bau-Biologie and Ecology

Color is also in the perception of the beholder. Some cultures have many names for shades of a color, as do native Alaskans for snow. Suppose one person can discriminate 150 different colors in total, but his or her culture has named only 50 of them. Some people have a positive or negative memory of a color based on their personal experience. In the end, understanding some basics of color and the meaning they are likely to telegraph is a good basis for choosing colors, for they express feelings.

The message of a color also depends on the color's saturation. Deeply saturated reds are different from those mixed mildly or markedly with white. Deep, midrange, and light are the three general categories of saturation, and each has a different emotional effect on us. Deep saturations affect us on a physical plane, medium saturations on an emotional one, and light on a mental or spiritual level.

THE MESSAGE OF COLORS

Color	Message
Red	Excites and causes a mutable energy
Blue	Centers and focuses us
Yellow	Makes clear and cheers
Green	Directs change and fosters growth
Purple	Provides a glimpse into that which is not known
Brown	Suggests stability and resistance to change
Black	Expresses mystery and absorption
White	Reflects possibilities and mental processes
Turquoise	Aligns us with our personal resourcefulness

Light and color provide 70 percent of what we experience in our environment and thus are key components in shaping spaces. Color is the detail that distinguishes form. Color sends emotional messages to our psyches by its tone, saturation, and the position it occupies in a space. The use of color can easily personalize a space or customize it to fit your needs.

Part III

Integrating Intangibles

Remedies for Clutter

10

Everyone has clutter. Even my mother, whose organizational ability is a legend among her peers, has some. Clutter is like a fast-spreading kudzu vine; it seems to multiply without any intervention, and the more you cut it back, the faster it grows. Cupboards, shelves, drawers, attics, cellars, and garages hold boxes, bags, and containers for the things we save intentionally, accumulate inadvertently, or just can't part with. And if these storage areas aren't enough room for the stuff we can't part with, it is mounted on hooks, piled in corners, or crammed onto shelves with a universal silent litany that we may need it someday, reuse it, or part with sometime in the future.

Why do we accumulate stuff we no longer have a daily use for? Certainly there is a biological basis for storing. Stocking up for times of famine or for the long cold winter is an impulse that once served us splendidly. But since we have a reasoning wizard, our neocortex, you would think that we could put this survival mechanism aside now that it no longer is critical to survival. Instead we seem to listen to the siren call of clutter and purchase a million different things. It's time to rethink this reflex.

We go on buying and buying and buying partly because we are convinced that we will feel happier, more satisfied, more fashionable, healthier, yuppier, with those trendy things we don't yet own. The fact of the matter is that we just don't seem to learn the lesson, no matter how many times we repeat this pattern in our lives. Stuff just doesn't have what it takes to make us happy.

It's fascinating to note that almost all feng shui schools insist that when an environment is altered, something inside you is adjusted too. Therefore, by clearing out clutter you can change your life. Furthermore, each category of clutter has symbolic emotional baggage. The sorts of objects you stash away have a meaning, and uncovering the underlying implication stored in the symbol may further your resolve to get rid of the stuff or organize it rationally.

In my book *Feng Shui and How to Look Before You Love: Techniques for Revealing Anyone's True Nature*, a great deal of emphasis is placed on how the objects you choose for your home, as well as the location you choose to place them, express who

> *"Any environment . . . should not become dominant; people are far more important."*
>
> JOSEPH ESHERICK,
> *architect*

157

THE MEANING OF STUFF

Kind of Stuff	What It Means
Stuff from childhood	Reluctance to accept adult responsibilities or inability to resolve childhood traumas
Clothing in different sizes	Lack of faith in self and low self-esteem
Outdated printed materials	Lack of faith in your present situation
Items bought but never used	Inability to find life's passion
Excess clothing	Desire for more love
Books not read in years	Ongoing search for life's meaning
Extra flatware, dishes, glasses, tablecloths or mats, and cloth napkins	Desire to please others
Gardening tools and seeds not used or planted	Inadequacy as a human nurturer
Nuts, bolts, and saved building materials	Belief that you still have much to accomplish in life

---

you are authentically. The same thing applies to clutter. There is a meaning not only to the kinds of clutter you stash away but also to the location it is in. It is no accident that you put things where you do. Consider the meaning implied by the location of your clutter to determine if you are willing to let it remain or take action to sort it out or build appropriate storage spaces.

On the other hand, in today's material world, retaining nothing tangible from the past can be a distress sign. I once knew a man who saved nothing from his past. No photos of family members, even of his children, and no memorabilia connected him to his immediate or distant past. In fact the only possession he retained from his marriage was a blanket given to him by his children. Keeping nothing is a sign of detachment and inability to be connected fully to others.

Your storage spaces and what you put in them should actually contribute to your life, and remodeling or building gives you an opportunity to design the kinds of storage facilities that suit your unique needs. In this chapter you'll find ways to plan for diverse storage needs.

THE MEANING OF WHERE YOU PUT YOUR CLUTTER

Location of Clutter	Possible Indication
Entrance of a home	Fear of relationships
Inside a closet	Resistance to examining emotions
In kitchen drawers	Resentment of or being overwhelmed by caretaking
Next to a bed	Desire for change or escape
On a desk	Fear of letting go or need to control
In a corner behind a door	Detachment from others
Under a piece of furniture	Importance of appearances
In a basement	Procrastination
In an attic	Living in the past
In a garage	Inability to actualize self
All over the place	Anger and self-loathing

Storage spaces to plan for might include the following.

Storage Needs
- Visible storage space for rarely used but valued objects
- Accessible storage for items used daily
- Places for seasonal things
- Places to keep things waiting to be used, sent as presents, or passed on
- Places for piles and other tabletop clutter

If you have not admired, used, or enjoyed an object within twenty-four months, in all likelihood you don't need it. Give away or simply toss out those things that make you feel as if you're wasting your hard-earned wages storing things that have no present usefulness. What is left can be stored in the following ways.

Visible Storage

Collections and redundancies like books, surplus dishes, and towels can add visible texture and emotional comfort to your daily life. In the same way that our ancient ancestors stored grains, meats, and other life-sustaining items for the winter or other hard times, we find comfort in knowing we have enough. Figure 10.1 demonstrates how underused spaces can be converted to storage areas.

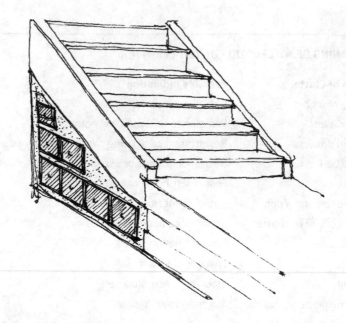

Figure 10.1 Space under stairs can often be used for storage.

ITEMS TO PLAN STORAGE FOR

General Items	Kitchen Items
Books	Daily dishes
Photo albums	Serving dishes
Towels, linen	Glasses, cups, saucers, and mugs
Toys	Canned goods
Collections	Dry goods
Trophies	Pet supplies
CDs, tapes, or records	Cleaning supplies and equipment
Files	Plastic containers
Computer software, floppy disks, and CDs	Flatware
	Serving utensils
Paper, pens, rulers, and other home office needs	Cooking utensils
	Pots
Household repair and maintenance equipment	Electric appliances (blender, popcorn popper, coffee maker, toaster, etc.)
Lawn and gardening supplies	Paper goods

Accessible Storage

Kitchen equipment, linens, towels, bathroom accoutrements, and clothing comprise the bulk of items that need to be stored accessibly. A whole industry is devoted to storing clothing, and, depending on your wardrobe, closet space should be divided to support the types of clothing you tend to have. I have a friend who spent a great deal of money renovating her closet and dressing table in her bedroom/bathroom area. The rows, racks, and drawers spanning the storage space intoxicated me with their promise. I fantasized about having such a clothes storage area and mentally tried to fit my things inside. Soon my mental charade ended, however, for I realized that I didn't have nearly as many shoes as she and she didn't have as many long dresses as I. It mattered not that this, by her standards, was the Cadillac of closets. I merely needed a Ford. In other words, until a bedroom, study, or other private space is customized for you, it will serve generically, like a hotel room, most but not all of your needs. If you have far more skirts and blouses than dresses, double-hung rods will be more efficient for you than a single rod. If you have as many shoes as the legendary collector of footwear Imelda Marcos, then floor-to-ceiling racks or boxes accommodating shoes will be sensible. Because no two wardrobes are exactly the same, we suggest you carefully consider whether you need more folding space than hanging, compartmentalizing (hats, stockings, handbags, and shoes), seasonal, or special protection. Figure 10.2 shows just some of the many options to consider when fitting a closet for maximum efficiency. With a great many options to choose from, it is likely you can put together a system tailored to your most specific needs.

Cooking Implements

The feel of a room influences our motivation to act. A cook's effectiveness and happiness is in part determined by how he or she feels about the kitchen. A poorly organized, dark kitchen that separates the cook from the rest of the family weighs on his or her feelings upon entering that space.

Nothing is more frustrating than having to bend, reach, twist, or go out of your way to extricate a frequently used item. Cooking utensils used daily are best placed within easy reach rather than tucked away where you have to fight cabinet doors and other impediments to retrieve them. Something as simple as hinging a door to the inside shelf of a cabinet that makes both the door open and the shelf pull out with one motion can be the adjustment that makes retrieving something easier.

A simple rod with hooks will keep frequently used cooking tools handy and reduce the nuisance of having to locate a spatula, knife, or peeler hidden somewhere in a kitchen drawer. You can bet on the fact that most famous chefs keep the tools of their trade accessible, and so should you unless your sense of order requires that nothing be in view. Feng shui's wisdom supports keeping everyday implements within easy reach so that daily work flows like a river uninterrupted by boulders. If you are annoyed, stifled, or just tired of trying to overcome an inconvenient daily pattern, then these remedies for common problems should be helpful.

Figure 10.2 Closets can be tailored to individual needs.

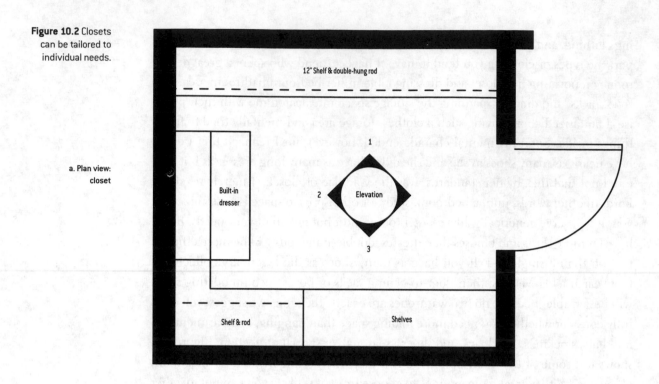

a. Plan view: closet

12" Shelf & double-hung rod

Built-in dresser

Elevation

Shelf & rod

Shelves

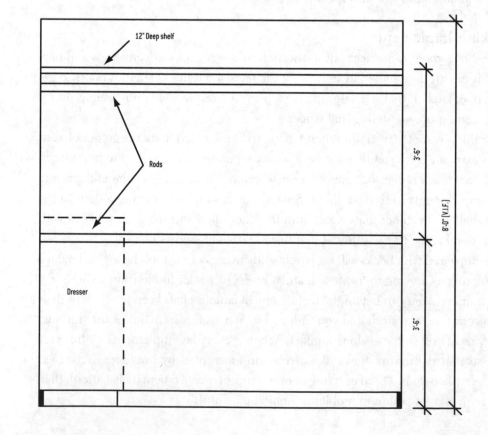

b. Elevation 1: shelf and rod inset

12" Deep shelf

Rods

Dresser

3'-6"

8'-0" (V.I.F.)

3'-6"

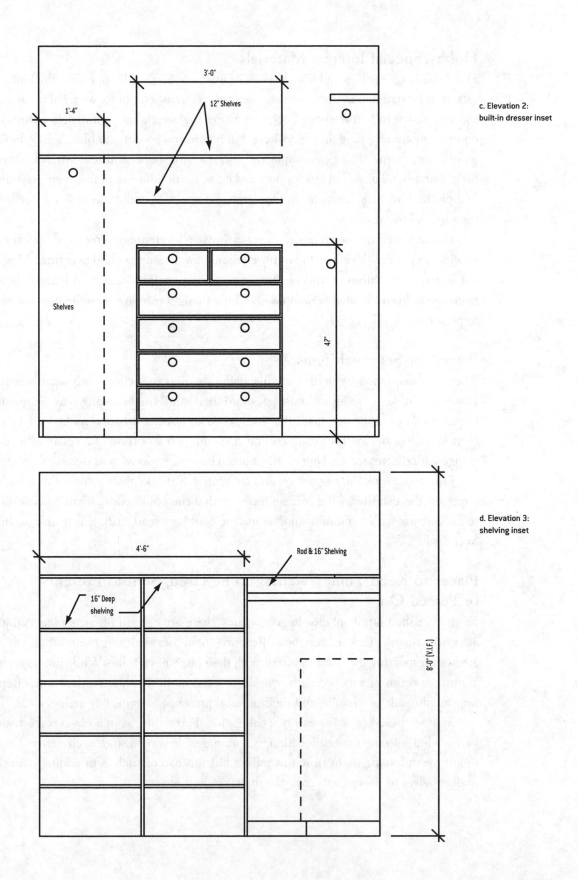

3'-0"

12" Shelves

1'-4"

Shelves

47"

c. Elevation 2:
built-in dresser inset

4'-6"

Rod & 16" Shelving

16" Deep
shelving

8'-0" (V.I.F.)

d. Elevation 3:
shelving inset

Hobby/Special-Interest Materials

From painting to golf, we all have hobbies or interests. Storage for our individual interests must be handled in the same way we would a cherished photo; we need to create spaces tailored to house what we require. Stores that specialize in innovative storage equipment are cropping up everywhere, but before you go out and buy shelves, look around your home. Things as simple as egg cartons for spools of thread, straw baskets for pet supplies, baby-food jars for nuts and bolts, small lidless containers for crayons, and plastic bins on wheels can fit the shape and size of a multitude of items needed for a special interest.

I once placed my stereo under a west-facing window that often received the brunt of windswept rains. Needless to say, my equipment was compromised over time. Musical instruments, albums, and electronic equipment might be served better when stored away from a heated or damp wall. A little thought can save those items you wish to preserve.

Places for Seasonal Items

There are many holiday items that, like daffodils, are experienced only once a year. However, unlike daffodils we must safeguard them until the following year. Seasonal things need out-of-the way space that is enclosed and free of dust and mold. Using the highest shelves in closets or cabinets and cordoning off a portion of a cellar, attic, or garage with shelves for stacking clearly marked boxes are two ways to store such items.

One client took this suggestion and ran with it. She also glued seasonal wrapping paper on the exterior of the storage boxes so that she could easily identify the contents, because with her diminishing vision she could not read writing as readily as she once had.

Places to Keep Things Waiting to Be Used, Sent as Presents, or Passed On

From cherished family photos to good wines, there are certain physical objects that are worth keeping for occasional use. Revering them means storing them in ways that are both respectful and commensurate with their place in your life. While photograph albums may not be enjoyed daily, weekly, or even monthly, their contents are often imprinted inside our minds, and their physical presence sustains our memory.

Storing these keepsakes can be challenging. Portability, as in a tea cart ready to be wheeled into the desired location, is a manageable way to store such items. That might mean having them stored in rolling bins instead of shelves or adding casters under shelves to move them easily, as shown in Figure 10.3.

Figure 10.3 A closet floor's storage accessibility can be enhanced by outfitting a closet with a bottom shelf on casters.

I store gifts waiting to be sent on a shelf in a closet reserved only for those things that I've bought all year long as they caught my eye. When an occasion arises, it isn't necessary to shop specifically for it. I am the envy of friends around Christmas and Hanukkah, for with very few exceptions I usually have my presents ready.

Handling Piles and Other Tabletop Clutter

If you are up to your neck in piles of paper, then this advice is for you. Bin it and label it! Telephone messages, letters to answer, ideas to think about, and bills are the labeled categories I have for my never-diminishing stacks of paper. There are probably some common features in that mile-high pile you have as well. Separating paper piles into categories will make the task of keeping up with the paperwork more manageable and can make the difference between just looking at piles of clutter and completing projects.

Linda Parks, a feng shui consultant from Chicago and clutter expert (see Resources), has these words of wisdom for decluttering for different age groups:

Young Children and Their Small Toys

Get rid of the giant boxes. Put Legos, Bristle Blocks, and other building toys in medium-size containers. It may feel easier to throw it all in one big one, but the reality is that the stuff at the bottom of a large toy box stays at the bottom, never to be seen again.

Children's hands are small, and their arms are shorter than ours, and smaller containers are simply easier for them to reach into. It is also visually simpler for them to identify what's inside.

For Teenagers

Teenagers are notorious clutter junkies. Make them a "stuff" box. As you walk around your home, cursing the stuff, just pick it up and throw it into the box. Don't put it away; don't take it into your teenager's room. Just throw it in the box.

Now you have a couple of choices for how to deal with this box. First, you can keep the box in your own space, hidden from your teenager. When he or she wants something that happens to be in the box, make the child pay you for it. That may seem harsh, but it can be very effective.

Another way of handling the stuff box is to give your teenager a limit on how long the stuff can sit in the box. When the box is full and the stuff has sat there for, say, one week, toss it. Again, strict but effective.

You may never change their habits, at least while they're living in your home, but you can remove teenagers' belongings from the family's common areas.

Children's and Other Family Members' Treasures

Finally a word about the scraps of paper, last year's birthday cards, the drawing of a child, or anything that has no equal and has no special space, including the stuff that grown children leave behind.

Everyone deserves at least one treasure chest—a box, drawer, or cupboard where an odd assortment of memories can be kept. I have a copper chest that stands underneath a dining room sideboard. It contains scraps of fabric, letters, postcards from travels, and those memories are far too dear to toss away. When the chest is too jammed to hold one more item, it is time for me to evaluate what is imperative to keep and what I can let go of. Would one dried prom corsage do instead of two? Would a few of my son's letters from camp be sufficient rather than one season's accumulation? Thinning out quantity and keeping quality is the goal. Most of these items are kept expressly to jolt memories, and redundancies will not change the content of the memories. A treasure chest bestows a place worthy of these remembrances' importance.

Storage needs are a fact of life, but we can and should be judicious about what we save and where. Will the scuba diving fins saved for the once-in-five-years Caribbean vacation be too brittle to reuse? Will the felt-tip pens run dry, the fragrance fade, the clothes fit or still be in style? What does time do to those items you are saving for the morrow? It is far better to be involved with the vibrant now than the completed past. When you lighten the number and amount of things you accumulate, you will find your present life less encumbered.

11

The Ba-Gua

Feng Shui Tool for the Emotional Divisions of a Space

The ba-gua is a feng shui tool that informs us about what specific human emotions are likely to be expressed in a given space. Like a map, it is divided into segments, called *guas*, that suggest the best areas for certain activities, furniture, decorative items, and architectural features. It can be laid over an entire home or individual rooms as a guide to building, remodeling, or decorating. While the concept of the ba-gua may sound rather arcane so far, pyramid feng shui has rational explanations for why the ba-gua's locations are associated with specific human characteristics. Because architecture places people in a space and provides a framework that suggests certain furniture arrangements over others, the ba-gua is a natural aid to any building or decorating project.

The ba-gua divides a space into nine sections, shown in Figure 11.1, but before you look at each of these individually, it's important to understand the broader picture involved. Start by looking at the ba-gua as a square room, with each of its sides, plus the center, standing for a certain area of life: the threshold is the motivation area, the side furthest from the entrance is the power area, the right side is the relationship area,

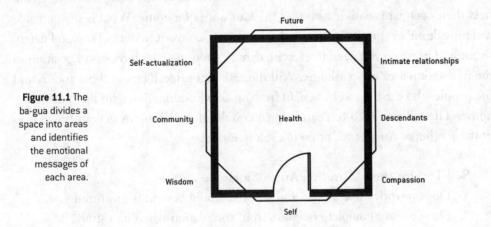

Figure 11.1 The ba-gua divides a space into areas and identifies the emotional messages of each area.

Future

Self-actualization

Intimate relationships

Community

Health

Descendants

Wisdom

Compassion

Self

> "... the architect who combines in his being the powers of vision, of imagination, of intellect, of sympathy with human need and the power to interpret them in a language vernacular and true— it is he who shall create poems in stone."
>
> LOUIS SULLIVAN, *architect*

the left side is the challenge area, and the center is the health area. Each of these is discussed in the following pages.

Motivation Area

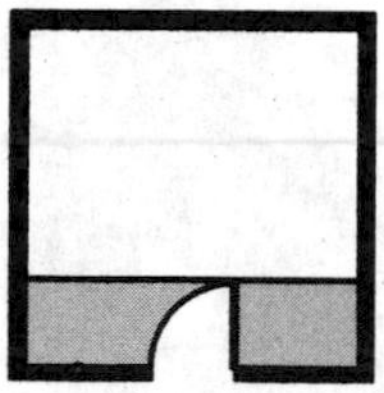

Figure 11.2 The motivation area of the ba-gua encompasses the wisdom, self, and compassion areas.

When you enter a space and are in a position to proceed into the main part of the room, look at the direction your feet are facing: this is the position you orient the ba-gua from. This is not necessarily where you take your first step into the room but wherever you are when you are facing the room's use area. If you turn naturally upon entering the room because a wall makes it impossible to move straight forward, or you find yourself drawn in a certain direction because you're attracted by a window, that's where you throw the ba-gua down. Where you are standing at that moment is the self area, which is the center of the larger motivation area shown in Figure 11.2.

The entire entrance wall and the three ba-gua sections positioned there make up the motivation area. First impressions are often lasting or at the very least hard to alter. The impression you get at the threshold of any space usually leaves a mental taste that lingers despite later messages. If you have ever been struck with disappointment or even alarm when entering a place, then you know how long it takes to reverse those feelings no matter what your subsequent experiences are. The threshold has the role of transmitting an appropriate message for a room or an entire home. What you see, how you proceed, and what is communicated furnishes a space with an ambience that fits or detracts from the space's intention.

Rooms in the Motivation Area of a Home

The main entrance serves as the transition space from the outside world to the inside and is usually placed on a home's street side. Likewise, rooms facing the street connect their occupants with life beyond the four walls of a home. What is seen outside will provide either stimulation or companionship or, conversely, distractions and defensiveness. Therefore you need to exercise care in choosing which rooms to position in the motivation area of your home. Will the activities undertaken in those rooms and the people who use the rooms benefit from an active connection with life outside the home? The following self-test can help you establish which rooms in your home may fit these criteria. Answer yes or no to each question.

Self-Test for the Motivation Area of a Home
1. Do you work alone all day and feel you would benefit from stimulation?
2. Do you want complete isolation from stimulation when in a study?

3. If cooking is a chore, not a joy, are visual distractions welcomed, such as watching passing cars, dog walkers, etc.?
4. Do you feel lonely or cut off from the world when at home?
5. Is a feeling of being protected from life's demands what a home can offer you?
6. Do you love having guests, but definitely don't want them to overstay their welcome?
7. Do you have teenage children?
8. Could your sex life stand improvement?

Answers

Here is what the ba-gua has to tell you if you answered yes:

1. A study would be good in the motivation area.
2. By all means keep any rooms such as a home office or hobby room away from the motivation area.
3. A kitchen or food preparation area would be good in the motivation area.
4. A daytime gathering space would be good in the motivation area.
5. Do not place a frequently used gathering space—living room, den, or dining area—in the motivation area.
6. Place the guest room in the motivation area.
7. Do not place a teenager's room in the motivation area of a home.
8. Do not place your bedroom in the motivation area.

In general, the rooms at the front edge of a home, facing a street's activity, are spaces in which it feels comfortable to be connected to the community. However, the motivation area's focus dissipates slightly about forty feet above the ground. Famed

---

WHICH ROOMS WORK AND DO NOT WORK IN THE MOTIVATION AREA

Rooms to Locate in the Motivation Area	Rooms Not to Locate in the Motivation Area
Foyer	Family bedrooms
Daytime gathering space	Family gathering room
Guest bathroom	Family bathrooms
Guest bedrooms	Family dining area
Kitchen	
Home office	

anthropologist Edward T. Hall conducted research discovering that at a distance of forty feet, the normal human eye cannot see enough detail on a person's face to form an emotional attachment to the person. Thus, those living in an apartment or condo on the fifth floor or higher (forty feet or more above the ground) feel less connected to people below seen from a window. However, a less specific but more encompassing connection to the surrounding neighborhood sights occurs. When I look out the window of my sister's fifteenth-story apartment in New York City, I am inspired by the excitement of the city. When I look out of my home's lower windows, the people I see, rather than the spirit of my town, motivate me.

Considerations for the Motivation Area of Individual Rooms

The motivation area of a room naturally relates to the room's purpose. The following is a list of things that might be in sight when standing in the motivation area.

Good Features for the Motivation Area of a Room

- A clear view of the area of use—the room configuration doesn't require furniture to be placed where its full visual impact would be blocked.
- A path to the use area that has no impediments—the room configuration doesn't require furniture to be sidestepped on the way to the use area.
- An enticing feature that lures people into the space—there is a view of an architectural feature such as a fireplace.
- No immediate jolt to the left or right—there are no wall or corner obstructions that force you to turn upon entering.
- A space for furniture or a convenient accommodation to the right of a threshold—rooms without a table, closet, or chair to the right of the entrance are perceived as less inviting than those with something to lean against or surfaces on which to put things down.

WHAT TO PLACE IN THE MOTIVATION AREA

Room	Item
Kitchen	Table to gather around, stool or counter to place items on
Gathering room	Cabinet with audio equipment or storage for appropriate accessories, table
Bedroom	Dresser, closet
Bathroom	Counter space
Home office	Counter, chair

Power Area

When we look at a space with defined edges (walls), the eye seeks light while, at the same time, discerns the scope of the room, diagonal lines, and movement. Therefore, when we enter a room we tend to embrace the depth view or focus on a window, a staircase, or anything that's illuminated, moving, or contains a diagonal line. Often the back wall of a room holds several of these features. Thus, the wall farthest from the entrance is experienced as the safest place, and for that reason it holds more power than other areas. The power area of a home or room is shown in Figure 11.3.

Rooms in the Power Area of a Home

In general, the rooms that are positioned farthest from a home's front entrance are the ones that should exude the feeling of privacy and safety. Because of their distance from the outside, they offer a sense of seclusion not felt in rooms closer to the front. The power area of a home sequesters and protects activities. Rooms located in this part of a home will be shrouded in a veil of privacy and security. On the flip side, though, they retain a detachment from community and outside activities.

In Arab countries a common building custom is to place all public spaces close to the front, with the rooms becoming more and more private the more deeply you get into the home. Apparently if you are invited into the rooms abutting the back wall of this type of home, you are considered part of the family. The following self-test can help you determine which rooms should be in the power area of your home. Answer yes or no to each question.

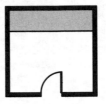

Figure 11.3 The power area of the ba-gua includes the self-actualization, future, and intimate relationships areas.

> **Self-Test for the Power Area of a Home**
> 1. Do you work best with few distractions?
> 2. Are there far too many pressures on you outside the home or from too many family members?
> 3. Does your family tend to wolf down dinner and spend far too little time engaged in table talk at mealtimes?
> 4. Do you and your mate spend a great deal of time separately without benefit of quality time together?
> 5. Do you want guests to feel welcome without encouraging lengthy or frequent stays?
> 6. Do several family members share a bathroom, with tension over its use?
> 7. Is it important to have family members cooperate with kitchen tasks?
> 8. Does any member of your family spend excessive time alone in areas other than his or her bedroom?

Answers

Here is what the ba-gua has to tell you if you answered yes:

1. A study located in the power area would serve you well.
2. A family room located in this area would help dispel outside distractions.
3. Locate your dining room far from the front entrance.
4. A bedroom located in the power area could improve your quality time together.
5. Do not locate a guest bedroom in the power area of your home.
6. Do not position a shared bathroom in the power area of your home.
7. Consider an area for your kitchen other than the power area.
8. Do not locate those areas far from the main activity centers of a home.

In general, try to place the rooms that have the greatest requirements for safeguarding in or near the power area of your home.

WHICH ROOMS WORK AND DO NOT WORK IN THE POWER AREA

Rooms to Locate in the Power Area	Rooms Not to Locate in the Power Area
Study	Guest bedrooms
Gathering room	Shared bathrooms
Dining room or area	Kitchen
Children's bedrooms	Home office

Considerations for the Power Area of Individual Rooms

In each individual room who or what occupies the power area will be imbued with authority and in some cases control over others or a situation. If there is no seating in the power area, the furniture, pictures, and other accessories take on a powerful role. For example, clients who wanted nothing more than to right a rocky relationship had placed on the power wall of their bedroom a painting of a lone man rowing in a storm-tossed sea. As we tend to observe what is on the power wall of any room first, seeing this picture when entering their bedroom only reinforced their problems. A serene picture of people engaged in a delightful situation, perhaps a picnic, would have better served them.

Good Features for the Power Area of a Room

- Cannot be visually blocked
- A limited number of compromising features such as pathways or doors leading elsewhere

- A beloved piece of furniture, accessory, or magnetic architectural element such as a fireplace
- Well-defined walls, floors, or millwork to make the area distinctive

WHAT TO PLACE IN THE POWER AREA	
Room	**Item**
Kitchen	Flexible workspace (not a fixed piece of equipment)
Gathering room	Space for seating
Bedroom	Wall space for a bed
Bathroom	Dressing and grooming area
Home office	Area appropriate for a desk

Relationship Area

The right side of a home or a room resonates with comfort and serves as a forum that supports connections with individuals. To say that the art of relationships and its concomitant rewards are important to a fulfilling, contented life is to say that air is necessary to sustain life. The relationship area is shown in Figure 11.4.

Why the Right Side of a Space Is Experienced Differently from the Left Side

At the entrance to an empty space you have the choice of proceeding inside or staying where you are. If you perceive the space as benign or seductive, you will naturally want to advance. You can proceed left, right, or straight ahead. It is human nature to head for a corner or a filled space rather than an empty one. If such spaces exist evenly throughout a room, then you are likely to veer right before turning left. Why is this?

Human beings are mostly right-side dominant. In fact, when scientists searched for the gene that might determine left-handedness, no such gene could be found. What they discovered is that left-side dominance occurs when an overflow of specific hormones are released during certain periods of fetal development. A person becomes left-handed not because of genetic makeup but as a result of biological events occurring during gestation. Most left-handed people actually started out as right-side dominant. As a consequence, left-handed people are still comfortable doing many tasks with their right hand, and, in fact, with respect to instinctive movement, most left-handed people react to many situations in the same fashion as their right-handed counterparts.

Figure 11.4
The relationship area of the ba-gua includes the intimate relationships, descendants, and compassion areas.

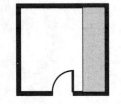

After entering and scanning the entirety of a space, almost everybody tends to move both eyes and body to the right. Therefore, in a general way the right side of a room feels more comfortable and more aligned with our natural tendencies. Feng shui tells us clearly that the right side of a room feels more natural for communication and camaraderie, while the left side of a room poses more of a challenge and is thus more suitable for self-generated activities.

In other words, the right side of a room is the appropriate place for activities that require cooperation or emotional support. In pyramid feng shui terms the right is the relationship side of a room and the left the challenge side.

Rooms in the Relationship Area of a Home

Rooms planned for communal activities are generally best positioned in the relationship area of a home. Since it feels more natural to proceed to the right, gathering spaces of all types stand to benefit from that position. Which gathering space your family members prefer to congregate in is the first question to ask.

In my grandmother's home the only true gathering space was around the kitchen table. As an immigrant woman from the last century, she found feeding her family the most satisfying way to express love. What little she possessed of material things she generously compensated for by the care and expertise of her cooking. In a world where money was scarce, appetizing foods were the gold standard. Distinguishing the haves from the have-nots was the airiness of her sponge cake, the subtlety of the fish balls, and the tangy and sweet mouthwatering flavors of her chopped herring. No other room could better encapsulate the essence of relationships than the kitchen of immigrant women like my grandmother. Which room in your home has this character? The following self-test can help you determine which rooms should be in the relationship area of your home. Answer yes or no to each question.

Self-Test for the Relationship Area of a Home
1. Do you and your mate have little time together alone at home?
2. Do you think it would be advantageous for your family to engage in more shared activities such as games, conversation, or simply any kind of fun task?
3. Are hurried mealtimes the only regular occasion for family togetherness?
4. Do you tend to hide away from other family members and spend a lot of time alone in solo activities with a computer, hobbies, or work?

Answers
Here is what the ba-gua has to tell you if you answered yes:
1. Your shared bedroom is best placed in the relationship area of your home.
2. A gathering space placed in this area may help.

3. Placement of the dining area on the right side of a home could be advantageous.

4. Placement of a hideaway room or home office on the right side could lead to isolation from family participation.

WHICH ROOMS WORK AND DO NOT WORK IN THE RELATIONSHIP AREA

Rooms to Locate in the Relationship Area	Rooms Not to Locate in the Relationship Area
Gathering room	Single bedrooms
Shared bedrooms	Study
Eating areas	Home office

Whether it's the family room, the library, a music room, or the eat-in kitchen, a home's right side must be the appointed place for family members to connect.

Considerations for the Relationship Area of Individual Rooms

The relationship area of a room is the most comfortable part of the room. It is the area we prefer to move toward when entering any space. Take advantage of this fact by placing items in it that are attached in some way to how you connect with others.

Good Features for the Relationship Area of a Room
- Ability to use the right side for conversation or any two-person activity
- Items that are shared, such as games, dishes, telephones, etc.
- An inviting feature around which people will spontaneously gather for conservation, such as a fireplace
- Surfaces to hang or place photos
- Nothing breakable or cluttered

WHAT TO PLACE IN THE RELATIONSHIP AREA

Room	Item
Kitchen	Dining table or serving counter
Gathering space	Seating at right angles
Bedroom	Bed for couples; play area in a child's room
Bathroom	Grooming area
Home office	Meeting space or visitor's chair

In general it is best to plan entrance doors for the left side of a room so that the flow feels natural. It is also advisable to leave out individually used furniture such as dressers or dressing tables that tend not to support the relationship area's intent.

Challenge Area

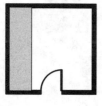

Figure 11.5 The challenge area of the ba-gua includes the self-actualization, community, and wisdom areas.

Since we are prone to shift to the right with both our eyes and our bodies when we enter a room, it stands to reason that turning or looking to the left requires an incentive if we are to assert our individualism. What is placed on the left speaks to the challenges we all face in forging successes. Thus the left side of a room or home encourages self-evaluation and personal growth. The challenge area is depicted in Figure 11.5.

Just as right-handed people have to reach across their plate to grip a fork, what we do on the left side of a space requires personal effort for which we often need extra support. A space for a single reading chair with an ottoman can be supported by built-in bookshelves, and a desk for homework can be supported by an appropriate task light. In a bedroom, perhaps clothes closets, a desk, or a sole chair can support its occupant's self-image, life experience, or self-improvement.

Rooms in the Challenge Area of a Home

All areas in which individuals pursue interests, learning, or activities that challenge are appropriately located in the challenge area. Since it is likely that the left side of a space will be used less frequently than the right, locating stairs in that area could discourage family members from using them. This means that a family that would like to steer members to the common areas could locate the stairs in the challenge area on the first floor of a typical two-story home to deter them from going up to the bedrooms.

Areas of relaxation or social interaction are less advantageous in the challenge area. Thus activities requiring one person's attention are preferred over activities requiring group cooperation. The following self-test can help you determine which rooms should be in the challenge area of your home. Answer yes or no to each question.

Self-Test for the Challenge Area of a Home
1. Are you driven to climb the ladder to success at work?
2. Do you forget to stay on a diet?
3. Are you likely to want to sequester yourself from common areas?

4. Have you enjoyed many successes that make you proud?
5. Are you competitive with a member of your own family?
6. Do you detest having someone look over your shoulder while you work?
7. Despite your achievements, do you still feel unfulfilled?

Answers

Here is what the ba-gua has to tell you if you answered yes:

1. If work success is still a priority, then a study on the farthest challenge side would serve your goals.
2. Be sure the kitchen is located on the challenge side of your home.
3. Do not place gathering spaces on the challenge side of your home.
4. A gathering room on the challenge side might be called for.
5. Do not eat in the challenge area of your home.
6. A home office would be less than successful on the challenge side.
7. Do not place your bed in this area or use it for yoga, meditation, or other forms of relaxation.

The challenge area should harbor the spaces where a comfortable expression of self-worth is appropriate.

WHICH ROOMS WORK AND DO NOT WORK IN THE CHALLENGE AREA

Rooms to Locate in the Challenge Area	Rooms Not to Locate in the Challenge Area
Home office	Room where games are played
Library or children's study area	Dining room
Computer area or nerve center	TV room
Bathroom	Bedroom

Considerations for the Challenge Area of Individual Rooms

All activity benefits from some challenge; thus there are appropriate items to place in the challenge area of any room. For example, if you are slow to select your morning wardrobe and get dressed, your bedroom closet and grooming area or bathroom would be best positioned in this area. If you tend to snack a tad too much, placing the refrigerator in the challenge area is a good idea. The following list recommends some other items that may be suitable to place in the challenge area of your room.

Good Features for the Challenge Area of a Room
- A desk
- A comfortable chair with footrest
- Bookshelves containing useful reference material
- Ample wall space to accommodate inspirational artwork and displays of achievements

---

WHAT TO PLACE IN THE CHALLENGE AREA OF A ROOM

Room	Item
Kitchen	Refrigerator, sink, or serving area
Gathering room	Reading chair, bookcase
Bedroom	Closets
Bathroom	Toilet (not in a direct line with the entrance)
Home office	Desk or visible recognition (plaques, awards, etc.)

Whatever nurtures the individuals or family to achieve their highest and best goals is appropriately placed in the challenge area.

Center of a Space or Health Area

One of the hallmarks of the practice of pyramid feng shui is that we seek patterns in the physical world of nature to support our theories. To understand why the health area is located in the center of a space is easy when we consider that most of our vital organs are found in the center of our bodies. The brain, the only vital structure not located in the center, is protected by a bony shield. Safekeeping what is vital is the mark of health.

All areas of health—physical, mental, emotional, and spiritual—are linked. Only with health in all areas of our lives can we transcend mere existence. Since the center of a space is well guarded from outside influences, it is natural to position things of innermost concern there. The health area is shown in Figure 11.6.

Figure 11.6 The health area of the ba-gua encompasses the center of a space and relates to well-being of mind, body, and spirit.

Rooms in the Health Area of a Home
Since the health area is located in the center of a space, what is placed there subconsciously feels most protected. That which is most protected takes on status or

importance. Thus the space that occupies the center of a home or the features that are placed in the middle of a room become by their position significant to the inhabitants.

For that reason it is advisable to avoid placing rooms typically used by one person—bathrooms, home offices, or hobby areas—in the center of your home. Common spaces such as gathering rooms and dining areas are appropriate. The following self-test can help you determine which rooms should be in the health area of your home. Answer yes or no to each question.

Self-Test for the Health Area of a Home

1. Do you spend more time with family members sitting around the dining table than any other place?
2. Would your day not be complete without relaxing in a gathering space, exchanging stories and conversation with other family members?
3. Is the bathroom the only place you can be totally alone in your home?
4. Are you regularly enticed to leave the family gathering room by a visible stairwell leading up or downstairs to private areas?
5. Is your home child-centered?
6. Do guests tend to overstay their welcome?
7. Are you often tempted to retreat to your home office, hobby room, or other isolated location?

Answers

Here is what the ba-gua has to tell you if you answered yes:

1. Positioning the dining area near the center of your home with a buffer such as a serving counter or cabinet stationed between any exterior window and the table will enhance the sense of community in your family.
2. The central position of this room in relation to all other rooms in the home can solidify core human needs of companionship, safety, and comfort.
3. It is imperative to create a space that feels just as vital to basic functioning as a bathroom. Therefore, do not honor this room's fundamental place in your life and do not locate it in a central position within a home.
4. Stairways within sight of gathering rooms' seating areas divert focus away from the heart of a home because of the eye's natural tendency to notice diagonal lines.
5. Placing children's bedrooms centrally in the home may create an inflated sense of their importance within the family hierarchy.

6. Locating a guest bedroom in the heart of a home bestows an inflated sense of belonging, making guests overstay their welcome.
7. Locating an individual's special room in the heart of a home disconnects and dissipates a family unit.

The center is the natural magnet in a home that everybody gravitates to and should be reserved for a family's most important shared activities. There is nothing more nurturing than being in the midst of loved ones engaged in satisfying activities. A home must embrace its occupants and guard them from feeling vulnerable and unconnected. The center of a home fills these requirements in ways that other segments cannot. Just as an egg yolk is surrounded by sustenance and protected by its shell, the central area in a home is the best place to harbor life's essentials that nurture human contentment.

For the sake of harmony, avoid or hide distractions like the diagonal lines of a staircase, disjointed architectural details, or many doors and windows. They all diminish the contiguous and embracing sense that a family's gathering space should have.

WHICH ROOMS WORK AND DO NOT WORK IN THE HEALTH AREA

Rooms to Locate in the Health Area	Rooms Not to Locate in the Health Area
Gathering rooms	Home office
Kitchen	Bedrooms
Dining room	Bathroom

Considerations for the Health Area of Individual Rooms

While the center or health area of a home feels protected, this is not true for the health area of individual rooms. We are more likely to place seating, the head of a bed, or a desk chair closer to the perimeter of a room. Seating ourselves in a room's center doesn't feel as secure as when we are backed by a wall. Therefore, we tend to ignore or place fewer things in a room's center. However, because this space resonates with our health, it is wise to make an effort to focus some attention on it. The following list can be helpful.

Good Features for the Health Area
- Any sturdy and useful item or room enjoyed by all family members
- Light highlighting an activity area

- Special flooring or an area carpet over existing flooring
- Room for both people and the kinds of supplies needed for enjoyable activities

We tend to take our health for granted until it is compromised. We all have experienced being unable to accomplish things well when feeling sad, or felt a gnawing sense of incompleteness when spiritually empty. Our physical, emotional, and spiritual selves must be fulfilled if we are to function at our best. Health is the staff upon which our life rests and feng shui offers a way to bolster it by tending to the health areas of our homes.

WHAT TO PLACE IN THE HEALTH AREA OF A ROOM

Room	Item
Gathering room	A patterned area rug or change in flooring
Gathering room	Space for right-angled seating
Bedrooms	A usable or compelling feature like a quilt at the end of a bed
Home office	Good lighting
Home office	Seating for visitors or a defined, patterned carpet
Kitchen or bathroom	Skylight
Kitchen	Work island or sufficient space for two people
Dining area	Dining table
Bathroom	An area carpet or change in flooring

The Specific Ba-Gua Locations

In addition to using the five ba-gua areas room by room as discussed in the preceding sections, it is possible to create an entire home based on the best positioning of rooms according to the nine ba-gua sections, or guas. Figure 11.7 shows our idea of a home that expresses the ba-gua in the most benevolent and highest way.

A ba-gua is like a psychological map showing how we tend to experience a space. Each segment has a specific emotional overtone that corresponds to rooms with certain purposes. The rest of this chapter goes through the individual segments of the ba-gua, except for the health area, which has already been discussed.

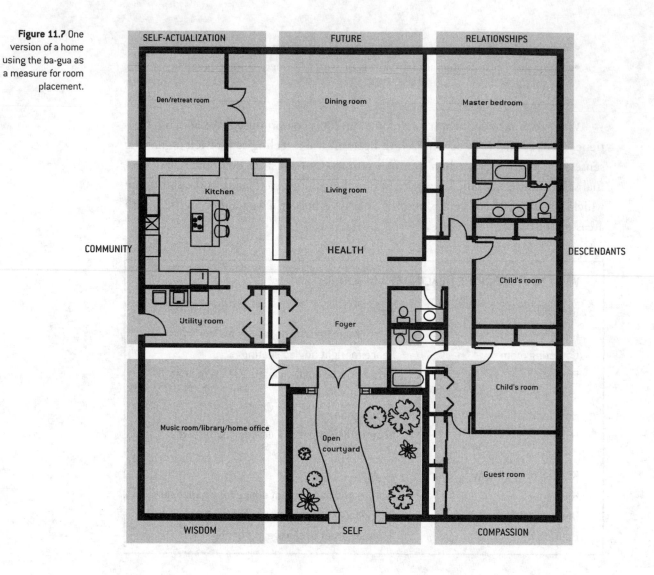

Figure 11.7 One version of a home using the ba-gua as a measure for room placement.

Self-Actualization (Upper Left Corner)

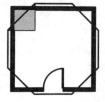

Figure 11.8 The self-actualization area supports self-esteem, which in turn supplies the substance for self-empowerment.

What person does not long for a chance to blossom into his or her personal best? The area of self-actualization or self-fulfillment is important to all family members. The upper left corner of the house and of each room, shown in Figure 11.8, should be dedicated to furthering personal empowerment. In our ba-gua home we have planned a hideaway room designed to serve the needs for fulfillment of each individual's dreams. In general, the self-actualization area is not the best place to locate conversational areas, nor is it a good idea to leave it empty.

As to this segment of a room, the self-actualization area can be fitted easily into rooms that serve one person—bedrooms, home offices, and hobby rooms, to name the most common. Do not place in the self-actualization area a second door or window that would impede the location of a reading or desk chair, a hobby table, bed, or furnishings that can support individualized activities.

Planning for the self-actualization area is more complex in common spaces. Activity centers that support more than one family member are the best approach for this area. Ample square footage with space for a table for homework or spreading things out can be one way to provide appropriately for self-actualization. Architectural features such as lighting, appropriate flooring, and adequate space to accommodate what is needed are the key.

Future Area (Center of the Far Wall)

The icon seen directly in the center of the back wall resonates with our hopes and dreams for tomorrow. The road untraveled invokes more fear than do paths already walked. That is, what we fear most is what is yet to come. Therefore icons that can be associated with dreams unfurling are ones that belong in the future area. The future area is shown in Figure 11.9.

In a home, a family's contentment can be measured by how they actualize their goals. To thrive in the present and in the future, family connections are essential. What room supports these connections more than a family space? For that reason we have chosen to locate a family dining room in that location. After all, it is on the foundation of this space that the Tao of family rests.

Intimate Relationships (Upper Right Corner)

What is more critical to overall contentment than intimate relationships? Without human connections, life would be lonely and meaningless. We need feedback from our kin, and therefore communication areas are suitably situated in the intimate relationships area, shown in Figure 11.10. Dining alcoves in gathering spaces, kitchen tables in kitchens, seating for two in bedrooms, and guest chairs in a home office are some of the ways the relationship area can be served best. Avoid solo activity centers in this area, with the exception of in a child's bedroom, where the bed, desk, or play area can be located appropriately in the relationship area.

The relationship on which a family is based is the couple that chooses to join together. For this reason we have chosen to locate the couple's bedroom in the relationship area of the home.

Descendants Area (Center of Right Wall)

We all want to be loved and to love, and there is nothing more rewarding than to feel as if we have something to offer the person we love. The descendants area of a space resonates with the desire to be of value to others and ultimately have something valuable to leave as a personal legacy. The descendants area is depicted in Figure 11.11.

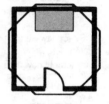

Figure 11.9 The future area holds the dreams we have for tomorrow in sight today.

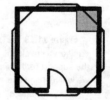

Figure 11.10 The intimate relationships area supports an environment in which human connections can thrive.

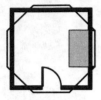

Elements that speak to this goal fit into this section of a room. Thus a couple's bedroom might have a niche for family photos. In an architect's study, albums of buildings designed or testimonial letters to the architect's work would be appropriate. Children's bedrooms in the descendant area are an obvious choice in the overall layout for a home. Should the occupants be childless or empty nesters, an office or hobby room in the descendant area would still be suitable.

Compassion Area (Lower Right Corner)

Another school of feng shui, black sect, calls this segment of a room not the compassion area but literally "helpful people." This traditional view implies reliance on others to assist us in reaching goals. No doubt we do need this help, but this interpretation does not underscore our personal responsibility for securing the love and interest of others. In general it rings true that you reap what you sow. Thus action or focus on what you can do rather than wait or wish for something to happen is the better plan. Pyramid feng shui suggests that the more caring and compassionate a person is, the more he or she attracts the help and guidance of others.

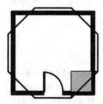

Because it is common to feel vulnerable and hesitant at the threshold of a space, especially an unfamiliar one, providing something for others to lean on when they enter implies compassion. What is placed on the right side of a threshold transmits the feeling that those who occupy the space want others to feel comfortable. The compassion area is shown in Figure 11.12.

Further, an entrance door should not swing open to hide the right side of a room. A window should not be positioned to the right of a threshold so that it would prevent the placement of a low table or chair. Coat closets, umbrella stands, and shoe racks are some other choices to consider for the compassion area.

Placing a guest bedroom in the compassion corner of a home is a good use of that area because it provides a caring location yet keeps the guests appropriately on the street side of most homes.

Self Area (Entrance or Center of Entrance Wall)

The entrance is at the juncture of our experience of place. How we are greeted in the overall layout or room by room is instrumental to our experience. Are we supported or thwarted? Each room greets us, and the lighting, pathways, and general ambience of the threshold set a tone that can be supportive or detrimental to how we feel about ourselves and the potential way we will use the space. The self area is shown in Figure 11.13.

Each room should have an inviting presence and each home a foyer that infuses those who enter it with enough emotional enthusiasm to feel welcome. The entrance of a home provides the transition time for each individual to slough off his or her public persona and slip into the comfortable attire of home.

Wisdom/Self-Cultivation (Lower Left Corner)

The left side of any space is less comfortable to turn to and therefore demands a greater effort to enter. To successfully meet a challenge, we have to dig deeply beyond comfort and embrace. This is the spirit of the wisdom area, shown in Figure 11.14.

Storage for books and important papers, surfaces to hold tabletop art books and ongoing projects, and drawers to house important papers and writings are the sorts of articles appropriate in the wisdom area of a room. In private spaces, choose items that give a physical form to an individual's potential. In a general sense, it's wise to place in the wisdom area those items that provide the individual with what it takes to climb the ladder toward his or her dreams. In a family room, it may be an activity center that serves all its members.

In the overall plan, the choice may be less obvious. Homes with their main gathering rooms in this position are saying the experience of home is difficult. Homes with first-floor bedrooms in that position also challenge the occupants' ability to feel secure. We chose a library for the wisdom position in the floor plan because a library is a communal repository for the knowledge that hopefully can be converted into personal wisdom.

Figure 11.14
The wisdom area supports those conditions necessary for us to thrive.

Community Area of the Ba-Gua (Center of Left Wall)

Our personal history plays a mighty role in shaping who we are today. The central section of the left side of a room is the community area, shown in Figure 11.15, and is aligned with our past experiences. These influences include family, community, religion, and nationality. In a very real way this is the genetic or karmic thread woven into our persona, the propellers that spin us into our future. We are an accumulation of all people, events, and places that have touched us.

Select items that honor those who shaped you and symbols that represent your wish for your personal legacy. Architecture can assist this. Each of us is influenced by holidays and those events in time that personalize our lives. A storage or display area in a home or room celebrating those events, occasions, or memories that tie us to the best of our past is an appropriate community icon.

Closets for storage of holiday ornaments, cabinets for Grandma's china, or shelves for family albums are some appropriate choices.

While you may be amused to see that we located a laundry room in the home's community ba-gua section, we have, by providing an exterior door, metaphorically acknowledged the importance of community, especially in households with children.

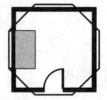

Figure 11.15 What is displayed in the community area underscores the support we have had in becoming actualized.

Providing a suitable area for children to enter a home without creating a mess acknowledges the community area. A closet for storage of holiday items, clothes that have been outgrown but are too dear to part with, and other belongings left over from childhood but not integral to the present are the threads that weave the design of our tapestry and are rightly placed in the community area.

Whether our ba-gua–oriented home works for you depends upon your specific housing requirements. What is most important to consider is how a room's placement and interior configuration aid or detract from the space's intention. You may be able to compensate for a room's inappropriate ba-gua placement within the home by highlighting that ba-gua area within the room, just as a person with severely compromised eyesight compensates by a heightened sense of touch.

Elements, Their Materials, Shapes, and Colors

12

Materials transmit messages. Everything substantial in the physical world is made up of only three materials. In feng shui we call these the elements of *earth*, *metal*, and *wood* (wood should be thought of as including all growing things and not just the substance of wood). All substances in the physical world contain one of the three elements or a combination of them. Even plastics are chemical and organic composites extracted from these materials.

Figure 12.1 shows elemental details used in building. Figure 12.1a has square windows, which are an earth detail. Figure 12.1b shows an arched entryway as well as a circular window. The arch and circle are shapes of the metal element. Figure 12.1c shows a raised-panel rectangular door with a horizontal rectangular transom. All rectangles, whether horizontal or vertical, resonate with the wood element. These three elements—earth, metal, and wood—are the elements that represent the materials we use to create buildings and furniture.

Feng shui describes two other elements, fire and water, that are not solid materials but rather the catalysts for change in other substances. Fire, the phenomenon of combustion, is an elemental force that acts on the physical world by transforming it. Water in its great abundance is present in the atmosphere and all living things and is constantly interacting with the physical environment. Fire and water bring other substances to their final form. All things are formed by at least one of the three elements and one of the two catalysts, for nothing is created without being manipulated.

Figure 12.2 represents the form of the catalyst elements of water and fire. Figure 12.2a represents a detail of a wrought iron banister. The flowing, curved lines replicate the water element. Figure 12.2b is a triangular pediment that is commonly used over doorways, which is a shape representing the fire element.

"Why anyone should think that marble is one bit better than concrete or that red brick is more human is something I have never been able to understand."

JOSEPH ESHERICK,
architect

Figure 12.1 The three content elements: earth (a), metal (b), and wood (c).

(b) North Shore Congregation Israel, Glencoe, Illinois. Designed by Thomas Beeby, 1982.

a.

b.

c.

Figure 12.2 The two catalyst elements: water (a) and fire (b).

(a) Handrail at the Hotel Solvay, Brussels, Belgium. Designed by Victor Horta, 1895.

a.

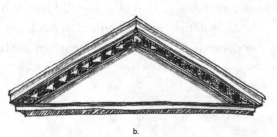

b.

The Messages Sent by the Elements

All shapes and colors are associated with one or more of the elements. A pitched roof sends a different message from a flat one; a square window is experienced differently than a rectangular one. On a home's exterior the relationship of the roof to the surface shapes like the windows, doors, and trim creates a picture that often has a strong elemental message. Indoors, much elemental communication comes from choices of shapes and colors for flooring, cabinets, trims, windows, doors, counters, and special features like fireplaces, as well as uncommon material choices for interior walls, such as stone and brick. Following is a list of which shapes and colors are associated with which element and what that element communicates.

COLOR, SHAPE, AND MESSAGES OF EACH ELEMENT

Element	Color	Shape	Communicates
Fire	Red	Triangular, pitched	Heat generating, attention commanding, forceful, active
Earth	Terra-cotta, brown	Square, chunky	Secure, low, safe, immovable, unchangeable
Metal	Shiny, silver gold, copper	Domed, circular, arched	Detached from the commonplace, elevating the mind's place in the scheme of things
Water	Blue, black	Undulating	Cooling, encompassing, boundless, make-believe, pacifying
Wood	Green	Rectangles, stripes	Durable, supporting, enterprising and willing to change

---

A structure can communicate a message based on its overall shape. The five sketches in Figures 12.3–12.7 will give you some idea of how an element's shape sends a message that is aligned with the element's personality.

Material

Shape is one way to communicate elemental characteristics, but using the actual materials is obviously another. The selection of stucco over wood for an exterior or glazed tile over natural stone for flooring is not only a matter of aesthetics but also a choice with emotional content.

Figure 12.3
A-frames and homes with steep triangular roofs communicate fire's drama and commanding message. This A-frame house, situated in northern Michigan, complements the cold environment by sending out its fire or warming message.

Architect unknown.

Figure 12.4 Architect Anton Gaudi's fluid lines align this roofline with the water element. Water shapes are organic and free flowing. Roofline of the Casa Mila, Barcelona, Spain.

Designed by Antonio Gaudi, 1906.

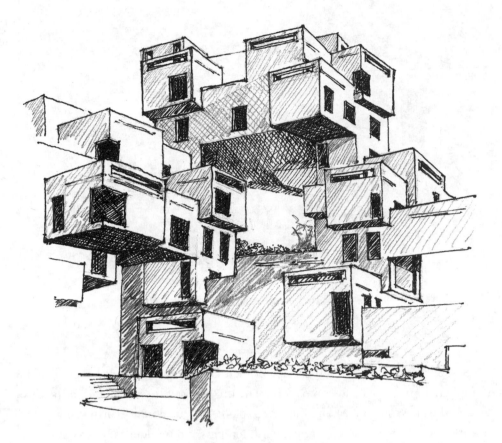

Figure 12.5 The rather square, chunky volume of this structure by Moshe Safdie is quintessential earth. Like a fortress, it appears to be permanently rooted in the ground. Housing Development Habitat, Montreal, Quebec.

Designed by Moshe Safdie, 1967.

Figure 12.6 Dome rooflines and structures send metal's message of transcendence from the commonplace while giving confidence in the human ability to figure out what is necessary.

Chapel on the island of Mykonos, Greece. Architect unknown.

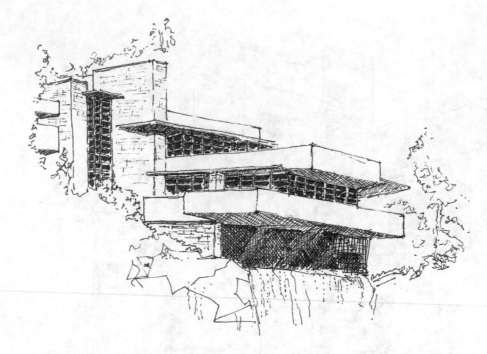

Figure 12.7 The many rectangular shapes of Frank Lloyd Wright's "Falling Water" capture wood's association with change and forward thinking. The name *Falling Water* refers to the use of water as an auditory and visual architectural element.

Falling Water, Bear Run, Pennsylvania. Designed by Frank Lloyd Wright for the Edgar J. Kaufmann family, 1939.

Sometimes materials and the shape of their content hold two messages. Take for example red bricks in a chevron pattern. The fire element is represented in the color red and the chevron pattern, but the material is earth. In actuality earth subdues fire, for earth cannot be burned; therefore earth tempers and moderates the fire message. Another example is a cedar shake roof. The color brown and square shape of the roofing are earth elements, but the material is wood. Thus earth's message of stability, safety, immutability, and endurance is mitigated by wood's message of being able to change. Thus combining elemental messages is like creating a good meal. It is necessary to understand nutrition and taste and include enough of both to make the food satisfying.

The following table is designed to show you how elements interact. The first element listed is the dominant element, and the next is the secondary one. Red, chevron-patterned brick would be an example of the fire-earth interaction listed first.

WHAT MATERIALS COMMUNICATE

Element/Material	Communication
Earth, unglazed tile, stone	Stability, safety, immutability, endurance
Metal, aluminum, copper, steel, gold leaf	Cerebral, not attached to the mundane, elusive, higher-minded
Wood, hemp, branches	Resilient, determined, able to change

If three or more elements are combined, their message is moderated. In the same way that a meal of a lamb chop, green vegetable, and potato has the nutrients for a balanced diet, a combination of elemental materials may create the perfect balance. However, at times balance is not the preferred state. Like an athlete who needs extra protein to sustain a marathon, we sometimes need to emphasize an element to support our needs.

MIXED ELEMENTS AND THEIR MESSAGES

Element	Interaction of the Elements' Messages
Fire-earth	Earth reduces the intensity of fire's message
Fire-metal	Metal intensifies fire's message
Fire-water	Water douses fire's message
Fire-wood	Wood feeds fire's message
Earth-fire	Fire enhances earth's message
Earth-metal	Metal restrains earth's message
Earth-water	Water shifts earth's message
Earth-wood	Wood reduces the power of earth's message
Metal-fire	Fire melts metal's message
Metal-earth	Earth enhances metal's message
Metal-water	Water wears down metal's message
Metal-wood	Wood acts as a point of reference to metal's message
Water-fire	Fire mitigates water's message
Water-earth	Earth almost obliterates water's message
Water-metal	Metal strengthens water's message
Water-wood	Wood holds back water's message
Wood-fire	Fire overshadows wood's message
Wood-earth	Earth supports wood's message
Wood-metal	Metal cuts back wood's message
Wood-water	Water supports wood's message

Although these relationships typically interact as described, all relationships are situationally based and are, therefore, perceived according to actual circumstance.

Building Materials

Let's take this information and look at its practical application. The selection of flooring, walls, ceilings, fireplaces, built-in cabinets, kitchen fixtures and appliances, and bathroom fixtures involves choosing materials. Their choice transcribes important emotional messages, yet we often make them in haste, after everything else is completed.

Flooring

Independent of material, the first choice made for flooring is to select between hard or softer, resilient textures. Hard flooring resonates with the earth element and communicates stability and safety. Earth floors are preferred for family members with neurological or eyesight problems. A soft, yet resilient flooring (a water element) might be preferred for those whose lives are often stressed.

Plank wooden floors underscore wood's message precisely, while parquet floors combine wood and earth. The first communicates exploration and fosters all kinds of pursuits, while the second advances cautious experimentation. Highly polished tiles combine earth and metal and cultivate comfortable mental activity. Unglazed Mexican tiles invite moderate activity because of their muted red, yet communicate a feeling of comfort because of their hard surface. Finally, soft wall-to-wall carpeting feels like the water element but the carpet's color affects its emotional read or elemental nature.

Walls

Drywall is the material used most often for walls. Alternative materials are typically applied over it. Drywall is fairly smooth (a metal element). The choice of paint, added to the metal element of the material, establishes the overall elemental experience transmitted by the wall.

Stuccoed surfaces are experienced like the fire element, while wood panels or paneled walls are clearly the wood element. However, if the wood is a brown color, the wall combines wood with earth, for brown is earth's color.

Mirrors communicate the metal element, while painted surfaces convey metal if they are glazed; water if they are marbleized; or earth if they are sponged with a square shape in a consistent pattern.

Ceilings

We notice ceilings only if there is a detail or light that draws our attention to them. Tray ceilings reshape a room, for they emphasize their own form. All pitched ceilings are aligned with fire, but those with a center peak have an even stronger identification with this element. Sometimes rooms have eccentric elevations such as a higher, yet flat ceiling over one area. Most of the time these ceilings resonate with the wood element.

Fireplaces

The fireplace's surround is the detail that furnishes the elemental nature of the fireplace. Most surrounds are three rectangles, a shape that is a wood element. Naturally, when the opening and the surround are different, their shape aligns the fireplace with the appropriate element. Stone resonates with earth; brown wood with earth and wood; light wood with metal; and metal with metal.

Built-In Cabinets

Naturally, the color of wood selected for cabinets makes a difference in their elemental nature. The darker the wood's color, the more it is aligned with earth. Light woods, especially those with a glossy finish, communicate the element metal. Glass inserts in doors give the items placed behind them more importance than the doors themselves, but if the glass is frosted they are closer to the water element. Finally, unless metal cabinets are treated to appear to be another material, they are aligned with the metal element.

Before selecting materials for kitchen cabinets, it is best to assess the cook's comfort with food preparation and the emotional significance he or she places on breaking bread with others. Earth elements are best for those of us who love, or want to love, cooking. For those who frequently dust and scrub their kitchens, the metal element conveys emotional detachment.

Bathroom Fixtures

A dose of the metal element will prevent people from lingering in shared bathrooms. But if you use the bathroom as a space to decompress, the fewer shiny or metal materials used the better, as the water element supports this need. The wood element supports paying more attention to grooming, while the fire element prompts sluggish digestion.

Materials, their colors, and their shapes are the elemental substances of all buildings. Knowing what messages they communicate can help us plan appropriately for our housing needs. Just as it makes a difference whether you wear silk or velvet to an August wedding, it makes a difference whether you choose a raised-panel front door or one with square glass inserts. This chapter's goal has been to help you make proper elemental choices based on your emotional needs.

Part IV

Inspirational Living Templates

Dreams and Concepts for Making Them Come True

13

A life without dreams is as flat as a sky without stars. We all need emotional hooks to toss into the future. Even the small changes suggested in this book will, we hope, get you closer to fulfilling your life's desires. But you should also have bigger dreams in mind. Toward that end, we offer in this chapter a collection of home concepts that, in total or in part, may help your grander dreams become reality.

Think of the concepts in this chapter as springboards. While someday we hope all these houses will be built, it is more reasonable to assume that you will reinterpret pieces of them in ways that are uniquely appropriate for you and integrate them into your plans. Like a well-tailored suit, a home should and can serve each inhabitant without compromising the ideals and goals of the group. Commercial plans may look good, but they cannot address those idiosyncrasies and nuances that separate you from the rest of the human race. The design templates presented in this chapter may not specifically meet your individual needs, but they are certainly outside the mainstream of commercial building choices. We'd like to think that they could be the impetus for your own spatial analysis and subsequent plans. (These drawings are intended as schematic concepts—remember that any structure built from these plans must involve building professionals well-versed in construction standards as well as local building codes and ordinances.)

Because the location of the house, the views from the windows, and the climate will vary tremendously, we have eliminated windows from our plans. You will want to decide on their size, orientation, and position based on your location, the intended use of each room, and your furnishings. We recommend, in fact, that you envision where your furniture will go before deciding on window placement in these or any other plans for a house so you get no unpleasant surprises. You may want to refer to two other books by Nancilee Wydra, *Feng Shui: The Book of Cures* (Contemporary

"A dream is but a reality waiting for articulation."

NANCILEE WYDRA

Books, 1996) and *Look Before You Love: Feng Shui Techniques for Revealing Anyone's True Nature* (Contemporary Books, 2000) to assist with furniture placement.

The Sunday *New York Times* of May 20, 2001, contained an article that stated, "The Census Bureau reported that fewer than a quarter of American Households are traditional nuclear families—married couples living with their children. Most people, then, are living in some other arrangement outside the boundaries of the old social contract." To respond to this reality, the plans in this chapter will work for varying living arrangements, such as unrelated adults sharing a home (we have called this group the Golden Girls), two families sharing a home (such as for two single-parent households), and homes configured to allow for boomerang children (adult children returning home) and those living with and caring for aging parents. The schematic floor plans we've developed for these categories are, however, flexible, adaptable for other needs too. While we suggest interior walls, standard door sizes, and closet/storage units, it is possible (and advisable) to alter them to suit your own requirements. A dining area without a partition from a gathering space can easily be adjusted to have, for example, a traditional fixed wall, an accordion wall, sliding shoji screens, or a low partition wall separating it from the adjacent area. While we have located the kitchen appliances, they too can be moved depending on view and personal preferences. For example, in many cases the sink is placed in front of a window. However, if on your lot that placement is not a good option, you can switch it with the stove or locate it elsewhere.

The plans in this chapter have been organized by size and relative cost. They all contain the usual requisites, from bedrooms to kitchens to gathering spaces; from foyers to garages to porches and atriums. Also, they all have been designed with pleasing interior views in mind, along the lines discussed throughout this book. As mentioned in Chapter 4, "The Parts That Make the Whole" a split eye, a long view that distances you from the room's main purpose or allows you to view an undesirable vista, such as a bathroom, is to be avoided. The view you will have as you travel from place to place inside your home, whether inside or outside, is a harbinger of what is in store for you, how you will feel in the space, and what you will be motivated to do. Therefore, as you adapt these plans to suit your own needs and desires, always keep in mind how your alterations will affect the interior views.

There are two elements, shown in the majority of the plans, that we suggest you consider incorporating into whatever design your dream dictates: the package passthrough and the nerve center or computer niche.

In Chapter 5 we showed foyers with pass-throughs for packages. With E-commerce so popular today, an increasing number of homeowners need a safe place for packages to be deposited so they are protected from theft and inclement weather and so the recipient doesn't have to arrange to stay home to receive delivery or go to some remote location to retrieve an undelivered parcel. You'll see these pass-throughs in several of our plans, but we strongly recommend that you consider including one in your own plans if you haven't already thought of doing so.

Likewise, we suggest that no home be designed today without accommodating the computers that are now, and probably will continue to be, indispensable tools in the home. Instead of sequestering the computer in a bedroom or having it disturb the look of gathering spaces, we have conceived of the nerve center (or computer niche) near the heart of a home to serve a family's technological needs while acknowledging its effect on aesthetics.

Further, these concept drawings have been categorized according to approximate size as well as relative anticipated cost. The cost is based on the design elements that would realistically impact budget—level of detail, complexity of shape, quality of materials, and craftsmanship in executing the design.

The Sundance House: Compact Modestly Priced House

The two-thousand-square-foot compact modestly priced Sundance House, illustrated in Figure 13.1, efficiently combines appropriate activity centers with a strong central and flexible hub. The name is derived from the period in adults' lives when they have more time for their personal needs and desires, a time when they are able to figuratively dance in the sun. Ideal as a starter house or a home for older people who want to continue living in a single-family home without the responsibilities of a large home, the plan wastes no space on a third bedroom, which would be used infrequently. Temporary sleeping accommodations such as a sleeper sofa or Murphy bed in the main gathering space could handle an occasional overflow of guests.

Similarly, we have chosen not to plan a second gathering room, such as a library or home office, for alternative activities because these needs can be served in the atrium, part of the dining room, or even the second bedroom if it is unoccupied. A nerve center is a must now that the computer has become not an option, but a lifestyle necessity.

Note that the central atrium/skylight area exists as a buffer between the private and public areas. The walls between the atrium and surrounding areas can be lengthened or shortened as desired to separate the atrium from the dining room and foyer or to open up the spaces. The atrium could also be used as an extension of the nerve center or fitted as a central hobby space (provided with hidden storage units) too.

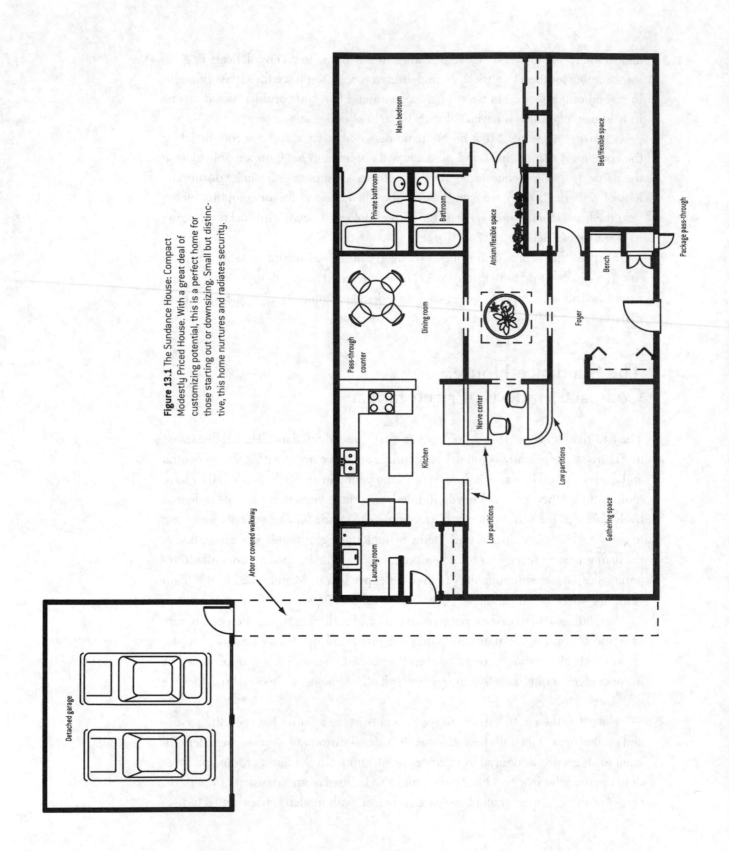

Figure 13.1 The Sundance House: Compact Modestly Priced House. With a great deal of customizing potential, this is a perfect home for those starting out or downsizing. Small but distinctive, this home nurtures and radiates security.

Detached garage

Arbor or covered walkway

Laundry room

Kitchen

Pass-through counter

Dining room

Private bathroom

Bathroom

Main bedroom

Atrium/flexible space

Bed/flexible space

Nerve center

Low partitions

Low partitions

Gathering space

Foyer

Bench

Package pass-through

While the home's square footage is modest, it feels as if the space is larger. The central atrium offers a variety of possible perspectives. It could be used as a traditional atrium, whose plants change with the seasons, or as a forum for art or other decorations that could be rotated. Such change is one way to enliven a space and re-create a sense of newness in it. This home has well-planned, customized storage units like a ship's galley, which stores many things compactly and efficiently.

While we suggest a detached garage in this scheme, it is possible to attach the garage, set back from the front facade on the kitchen side of the house. The back entrance could stay where it is, accessed from the garage instead of the yard, because there is still a formal entrance in front.

The Diamond Domicile: Compact Higher-Priced House

While still compact at about twenty-five hundred square feet, the additional space in this higher-end house, shown in Figure 13.2, allows for more flexibility. Like a diamond, this small but exquisitely designed house takes facets of space and reinterprets them. With a higher budget, you could also add a great deal of customized details. For example, the nerve center's low partition can be fashioned from an exotic wood. The kitchen drawers can be customized and accessorized to accommodate even the most discriminating gourmet. Electronic controls for sound, media, temperature, and window coverings could assist in setting a myriad of scenes throughout the day, based on use. There are a growing number of home systems that clean air, dispense fragrances, and control lighting that can be factored into this plan.

This plan has our package pass-through as well as a central nerve center. The screened porch could be another office, music or media room, or alternative flex space. Note the proximity of the nerve center to the kitchen and heart of the home. Should there be need for a home business requiring employees, what is shown as a garage could easily be converted to such a business space with a separate entrance.

The Sequoia House: Medium-Size Modestly Priced House

Sequoia trees grow to great heights. Our Sequoia House is designed to support the potentially limitless magnitude of the human spirit. Shown in Figure 13.3, it is a reasonably priced four-bedroom house with about three thousand square feet of space.

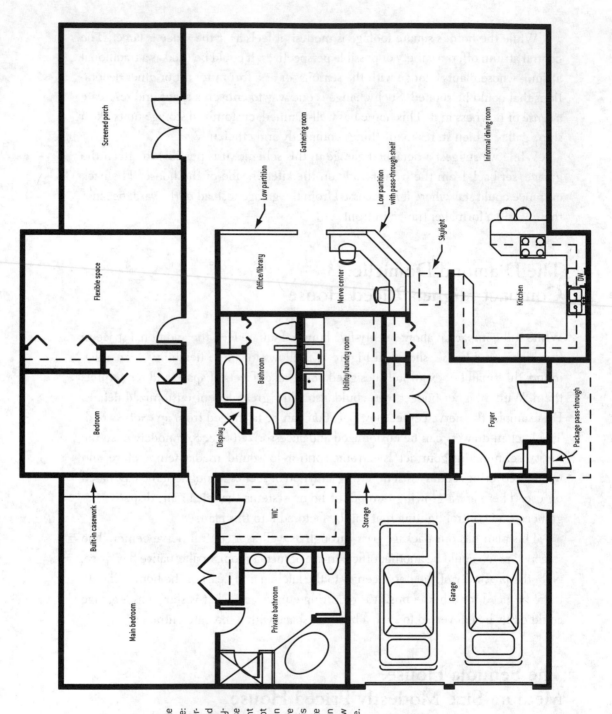

Figure 13.2 The Diamond Domicile: Compact Higher-Priced House. A good choice for empty-nesters or those living solo who want quality but not quantity. An option for creative customization, this easy-to-negotiate space is high on possibilities and low on maintenance.

Screened porch

Flexible space

Low partition

Gathering room

Informal dining room

Office/library

Low partition with pass-through shelf

Nerve center

Skylight

Kitchen

DW

Bathroom

Utility/laundry room

Display

Bedroom

Foyer

Package pass-through

Built-in casework

WIC

Storage

Main bedroom

Private bathroom

Garage

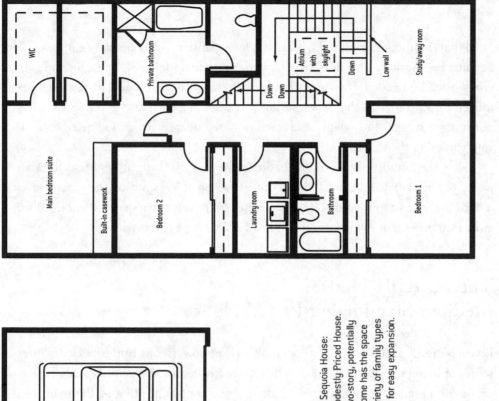

Second-floor plan

Figure 13.3 The Sequoia House:
Medium-Size Modestly Priced House.
This effective two-story, potentially
four-bedroom home has the space
needed for a variety of family types
and is designed for easy expansion.

First-floor plan

Note that this model's footprint is also ideal for expansion. The one-story garage could become two stories with a flexible hobby/media space upstairs. Should a second gathering space be needed, the garage space could be used, and a new garage could be moved forward toward the main entrance. If built as shown and if vehicular access permits, we suggest the garage be entered from the side, thus creating space for a private garden to the side of the house.

Note the laundry area is on the bedroom level and a skylight brightens the stairwell. We have labeled the fourth bedroom, at the top of the stairs on the second level, a study/away room to show that it could be used for private extra space or a home office away from the main living level if you need only three bedrooms.

The Butterfly House:
Medium-Size Higher-Priced House

Like a butterfly's ability to alight on a multitude of flowers, our Butterfly House offers scores of living options. What makes this thirty-five-hundred-square-foot plan appropriate for a couple or an adult living alone is the central position of the main bedroom. Too often floor plans tuck the main bedroom away from the heart of the home. In this home, shown in Figure 13.4, privacy is not an issue; rather centrality is a desired asset. This plan's circulation guards against having any one area underused.

The gracious foyer leading into a hallway/reception hub off the public spaces is designed to provide privacy for the home's main use areas. The ample wall space in the hallway transforms a passageway into a potential art gallery. The floor space outside the office/study/library avails those entering a sweeping visual of the home's main gathering space. It is conceivable to locate a round skylight or a podium for a favorite sculpture here to reinforce the options for circulation. Should one member of this household be wheelchair-bound, this ample space makes changing direction to roam through the house a snap.

Other features include:

- Commodious storage spaces in front foyer, back hallway, and guest bedrooms, precluding the owners from having to mount steps into a basement or attic to store items
- A special feature (either a two-way fireplace or a water feature wall) in the main bedroom
- Built-in seating or sauna/steam area off the tub/shower
- Package pass-through

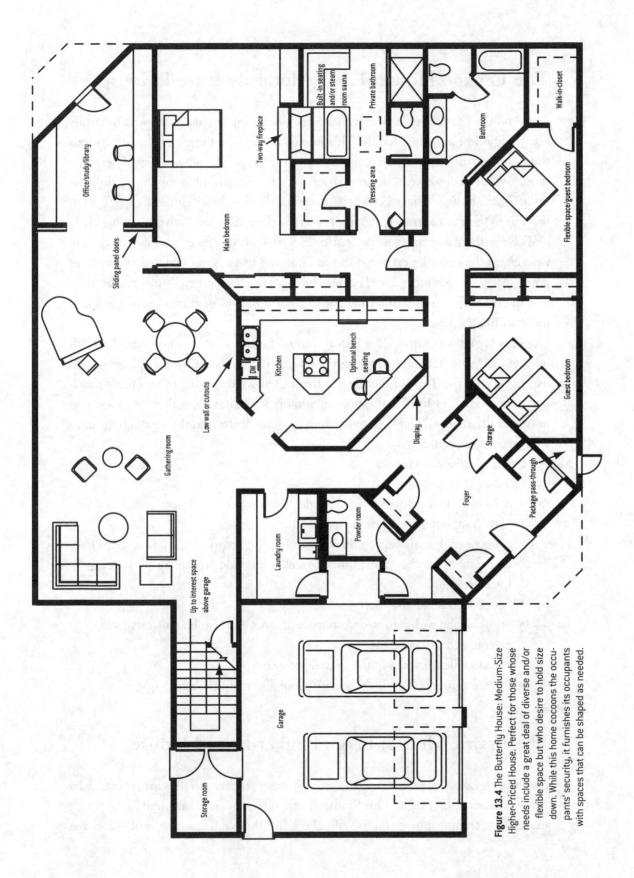

Figure 13.4 The Butterfly House: Medium-Size Higher-Priced House. Perfect for those whose needs include a great deal of diverse and/or flexible space but who desire to hold size down. While this home cocoons the occupants' security, it furnishes its occupants with spaces that can be shaped as needed.

The Ginkgo House: Large Modestly Priced House

Based on the age-old tree that is its namesake, our Ginkgo House supports the time-less tradition of a nuclear family. This home's layout (see Figure 13.5), with its four thousand square feet of space, could cater to the needs of numerous lifestyles. The ground-floor bedroom can serve as space for an aging parent, boomerang child, or home-based business that receives clients. Since the first floor's gathering space is farthest from the front entrance, the front two rooms are afforded a privacy not normally available without a separate entrance. However, if a private office entrance is required, we suggest the room be extended forward into the space now occupied by the front porch. A separate entrance could be positioned off the front porch. Further, that room and the other front room (informal gathering space) can function as separate apartment within the home.

This layout was inspired by a story from a former student whose aging grandmother lived with her family. This ninety-six-year-old woman was hard of hearing and had to turn up the TV to a sound level that just about drove the other family members crazy. Had they lived in this housing prototype, their main gathering area would have had the stairwell and hallway acting as a noise buffer and their gathering space would have been quiet.

Other lifestyle features are:

- A second-floor gathering space available to serve current needs such as a playroom, hobby, or exercise area
- A nerve center adjacent to the kitchen but not the main gathering space that can serve as another home office as well as provide privacy for those using the computer
- Second-floor laundry room
- Study/hobby niches in two upstairs bedrooms that can be converted into customized storage areas
- Private toilet/tub area in the shared bathroom
- Private garden areas off the ground floor and main gathering spaces

The Prairie House: Large Higher-Priced House

Creatures residing on prairies live in vastly different arenas—on the earth's surface by day and beneath it at night. Our Prairie House offers its residents public spaces that are separate from its private ones. With about five thousand square feet of space, the

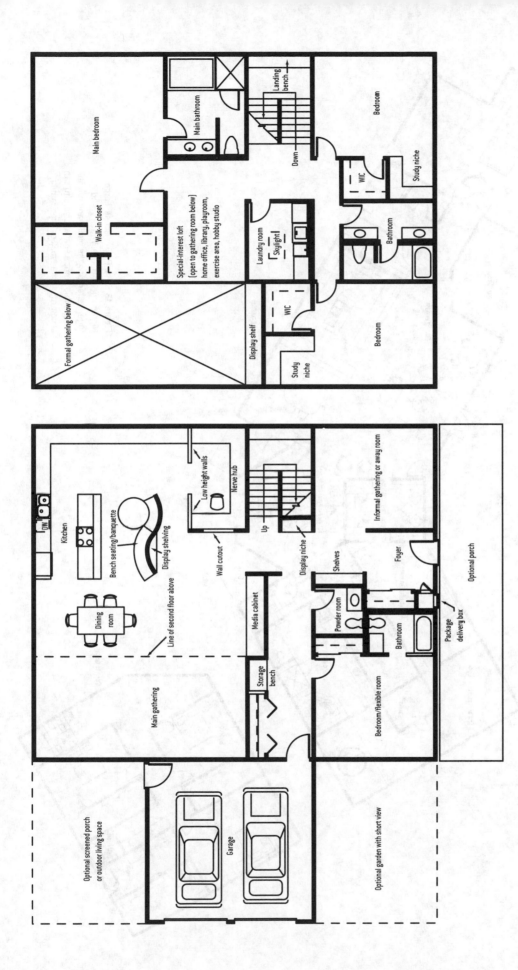

Figure 13.5 The Ginkgo House: Large Modestly Priced House. When the size of a lot allows for a larger footprint, inventive spatial planning can be implemented with fewer constraints . This home is uniquely designed for boomerang children, caretaking of aging parents, or a customer-based home business.

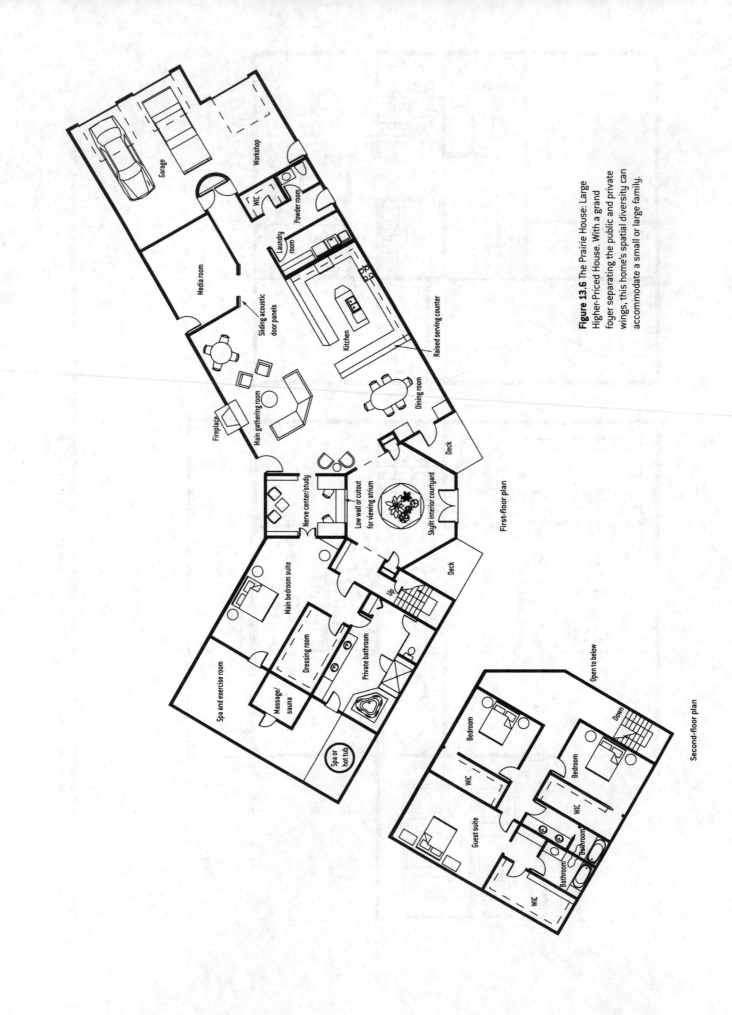

Figure 13.6 The Prairie House: Large Higher-Priced House. With a grand foyer separating the public and private wings, this home's spatial diversity can accommodate a small or large family.

Garage

Workshop

WIC

Powder room

Laundry room

Media room

Sliding acoustic door panels

Kitchen

Fireplace

Main gathering room

Dining room

Raised serving counter

Deck

Nerve center/study

Low wall or cutout for viewing atrium

Skylit interior courtyard

Deck

First-floor plan

Main bedroom suite

Spa and exercise room

Massage/sauna

Dressing room

Private bathroom

Spa or hot tub

Up

Guest suite

WIC

Bedroom

WIC

Bedroom

Bathroom

WIC

Bathroom

Down

Open to below

Second-floor plan

plan shown in Figure 13.6 has the potential to answer many different lifestyle needs. This home can easily serve a family with children or a couple whose children have moved away and return only to visit. All ground-level rooms have the potential for exterior access. The central atrium feels more like a meeting zone than a hallway delivering occupants to different areas. It also serves as a buffer zone between the public and private spaces.

The nerve center/study area is another special hub. With access from the main bedroom as well as the public space, this creates circulation options for the home's main occupants, who, we believe, would naturally choose this bedroom. Installing a low wall between this and the foyer atrium makes the nerve center/study seem larger because of the view into the atrium foyer. Moreover, we feel that a feature as visually significant as an atrium should have as much use (visually and with regard to circulation) as possible.

The second and third bedrooms could work as offices for home businesses as well, for they are adequately sequestered from the living areas. As with many of our schematic designs, the secondary bedroom area could be added on as a wing on the main level. If these bedrooms were added as a single-level wing, a secondary entrance to the front of the home would be possible and could benefit some lifestyle needs.

If this home were to be built in a warm climate, the gathering room's fireplace could be eliminated and replaced with either a wall of glass or a water feature.

While we do not show a casual breakfast area in the kitchen, building a multilevel island with a space for a dining-height counter allows for seating that can be used for casual dining. Also, a barlike counter could be installed between the kitchen and the gathering spaces for a variety of options for "perching" spaces. Another possibility for this counter is a traditional bar built facing the gathering space.

Other special features are:

- A more flexible double-door entrance from the garage
- Garage workspace or a three-car garage
- Sauna, spa, and exercise area off the main bedroom
- A powder room accessible to the gathering spaces and main circulation path, while being visually tucked away

The Golden Girls Habitat

Many adults, through divorce or the death of a spouse, are living alone. Often they find themselves unprepared for the expense and hassle of maintaining a residence by themselves. The television program "The Golden Girls" promotes an alternative to living alone—that of clustering a few adults, not necessarily related, under one roof. For many sharing a home is the only way to maintain the level and cost of individual housing commensurate with their former lifestyle. Our plan, shown in Figure 13.7, provides private bedroom suites, a large enough kitchen for several adults to share as co-cooks, and common as well as individual niches for messages, packages, and mail— within a total of about thirty-five hundred square feet of space.

The foyer plays an important role as both a station for removing outerwear and a mail/communication center. A mail table is large enough to accommodate an answering machine and a message board for house members to communicate.

In many ways each adult's bedroom door is a secondary front door, for it is the gateway to his or her personal space. Installing niches next to each bedroom's doors not only creates a personal drop-off area but also provides space for each individual to customize his or her entrance. These interior thresholds (bedroom doors) should serve as does a home's front door and communicate each occupant's personality.

In a home occupied by several unrelated adults we think it is a benefit to have several optional-use spaces. Since one's bedroom is not always the optimum location for visitors, we have designed several optional-use spaces to serve a variety of guests, from grandchildren to special friends. A feature like a window seat on the stairwell landing is one example, as is the skylit interior hub on the second floor. The computer room could have a pocket door, and the laundry/lounge could have a sliding wall concealing the utility area to expand the optional-use opportunities for these areas.

Further, the rather large gathering area permits flexible seating groups, as illustrated by the swivel chairs between the piano and the sofas.

In the kitchen, the stools perched at the end of the island prevent guests from being underfoot without denying them conversation access to the cook or cooks. Having two sinks is a must in a kitchen used by potentially two or more persons.

An efficient library serves all occupants at one time should they want to work concurrently at the computer stations. Naturally this house should comply with the requirements of the Americans with Disabilities Act (ADA) for living barrier free. Notice we have provided a location for a vertical lift.

The New Two-Family House

This plan, which provides seventeen hundred square feet of common space as well as thirteen hundred square feet of private space in each of two separate pods, can answer the needs of the swelling ranks of single adults raising children. Sharing a central core and still retaining independent sleeping/gathering units can lessen each family's workload, child-care, and fiscal responsibilities. Other alternative groups might be work-

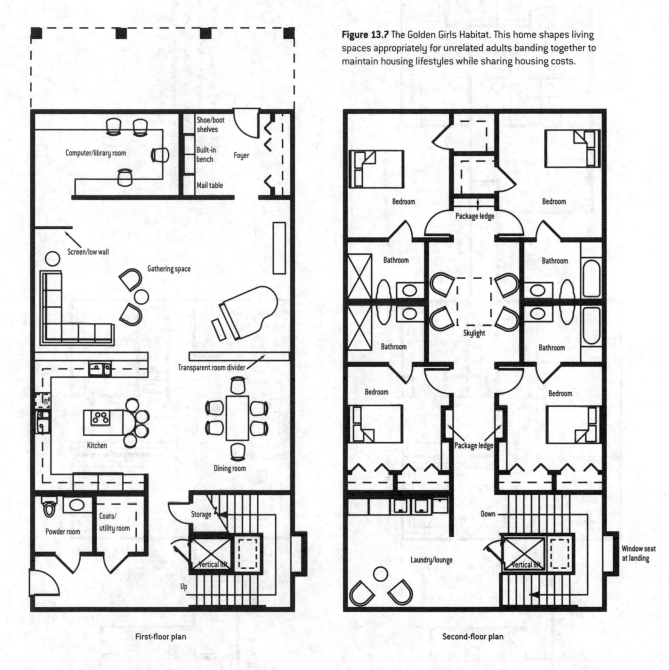

Figure 13.7 The Golden Girls Habitat. This home shapes living spaces appropriately for unrelated adults banding together to maintain housing lifestyles while sharing housing costs.

First-floor plan

Second-floor plan

ing couples with aging parents or close friends or siblings wanting to share costs and responsibilities of raising children. While our concept is designed for two families, as shown in Figure 13.8, it can be expanded to serve more.

The commodious central space includes common facilities for food preparation, dining, laundry, package pass-through, workshop, computer nerve center, and gathering. In other words all public spaces are common, although each private pod has its own smaller gathering space.

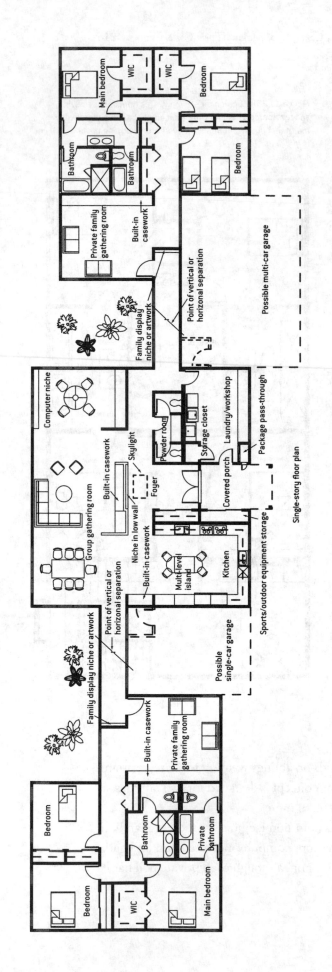

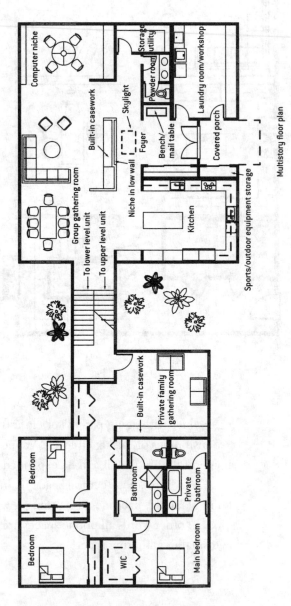

Figures 13.8 The New Two-Family House. Designed to lighten the economic and social burden for single-parent families, this home deviates from the traditional two-family home by sharing most public spaces. Each family has its own private pod.

Single-story floor plan

- Bathroom
- Main bedroom
- WIC
- WIC
- Bedroom
- Private family gathering room
- Built-in casework
- Bedroom
- Computer niche
- Group gathering room
- Built-in casework
- Skylight
- Foyer
- Niche in low wall
- Built-in casework
- Multi-level island
- Kitchen
- Powder room
- Storage closet
- Laundry/workshop
- Package pass-through
- Covered porch
- Sports/outdoor equipment storage
- Point of vertical or horizontal separation
- Family display niche or artwork
- Possible multi-car garage
- Possible single-car garage
- Private family gathering room
- Bedroom
- Bedroom
- Bathroom
- Private bathroom
- WIC
- Main bedroom

Multistory floor plan

- Bedroom
- Private family gathering room
- Built-in casework
- Bathroom
- Private bathroom
- WIC
- Main bedroom
- To lower level unit
- To upper level unit
- Group gathering room
- Computer niche
- Built-in casework
- Skylight
- Foyer
- Niche in low wall
- Kitchen
- Bench/mail table
- Powder room
- Storage/utility
- Laundry room/workshop
- Covered porch
- Sports/outdoor equipment storage

Entrances from the garages give a family the option to enter either the private or public spaces while the front entrance leads into the common areas only. If a single level is used, each family is afforded a private garden that can be reached by installing another door in the connecting hallway. If more storage is needed, the connecting hallway can be widened to accommodate a long wall of closets.

Final Thoughts

It is certainly not the intention of this book to dictate how to live. Feng shui, in fact, encourages us to recognize our core needs and not be guided by the flavor of the month in building styles. We all have experienced a building type that is hot for a period of time until another design replaces it. Housing design should serve function; your desires and dreams should never be forced to submit to the constraints of form and style.

The amount of time spent conscientiously planning a space will reap rewards far greater than you can imagine. A well-thought-out space can eliminate daily inconveniences and annoyances. Your home can be the catalyst to attract all that you wish to have. We leave you with tools for building and remodeling a home and know that they also will serve to shape your life.

Afterword

We Are Our Surroundings

As the human species advances, there is a breakdown in differential functioning. That is, as we advance and are freed more and more from attending to self-preservation, many of the things we once did for ourselves are handled otherwise. This delegation of survival tasks has pushed evolution forward. Without shelter, the human species would never have proliferated and certainly would have been limited geographically to warmer climates.

Evolution has also been moved ahead whenever we have eliminated discontinuities from our view of the universe. Walter Anderson writes in his revealing book *Evolution Isn't What It Used to Be: The Augmented Animal and the Whole Wired World*:

> Human evolutionary progress is a story of lessons learned—lessons of a very specific kind: with each lesson the human species discovers that things once taken to be separate are not that at all. . . . We learned the Copernican lesson that our planet is not discontinuous from the heavenly bodies, we learned the Darwinian lesson that humans are not discontinuous from the animals, and we learned the Freudian lesson that the conscious mind is not discontinuous from its preconscious origins.

From the ashes of the World Trade Center rose a new awareness in Americans of how vital place is to our feelings, our experience, our quality of life. We are guided by a subconscious mind that interprets its surroundings. More and more we understand on a profoundly deep level that we as living beings are not discontinuous from our environment. Our wish is that this book has given you tools that will help you embrace your intimate connection with the place in which you live, to weave the messages of place into your life. Our homes give us the opportunity to craft spaces that are truly satisfying sanctuaries—both emotionally and physically. Using the feng shui concepts

"If clothing is an extension of our private skins to store and channel our own heat and energy, housing is a collective means of achieving the same thing for the family or the group. Housing as shelter is an extension of our bodily heat-control mechanism—a collective skin or garment."

MARSHALL MCLUHAN,
educator

in this book, we can design environments that nurture and protect the human spirit while providing the very basic function of protective physical shelter.

What shelter is in its most basic form is an expression of how we live. While we create shelter, it creates us. Since shelter and its elaborate schemes are a reflection of how we believe life should be lived, every choice becomes important to fulfilling our desires. When choosing the structure and the details that will mold your life, do so with the utmost consciousness.

Resources

Books

Ackerman, Diane, *A National History of the Senses*. New York: Random Value Publishing, 1990.

Alexander, Christopher, Ishikawa, Sara, and Silverstein, Murray. *A Pattern Language: Towns, Buildings, Construction*. New York: Oxford University Press, 1977.

American Institute of Architects. *Design for Aging: An Architect's Guide*. Washington, D.C.: AIA Press, 1985.

Anderson, Walter Truett. *Evolution Isn't What It Used to Be: The Augmented Animal and the Whole Wired World*. New York: W.H. Freeman, 1997.

Birren, Faber. *Color Psychology and Color Therapy*. Secaucus, NJ: Citadel Press, 1961.

Bloomer, Kent C., and Moore, Charles W. *Body, Memory, and Architecture*. New Haven, CT.: Yale, 1977.

Campbell, Don. *The Mozart Affect*. New York: Avon Books, 1997.

Ching, Francis D. K. *Architecture: Form—Space & Order*. Bethesda, MD: Van Nostrand Reinhold Company, 1979.

Costantino, Maria. *Gaudi*. Edison, NJ: Chartwell Books, 1993.

Curtis, William J.R. *Le Corbusier, Ideas and Forms*. New York: Rizzoli International Publications, 1986.

Gallagher, Winifred. *Power of Place: How Our Surroundings Shape Our Thoughts, Emotions, and Actions*. New York: Simon and Schuster, 1993.

Gallagher, Winifred. *Working on God*. New York: Random House, 1999.

Guthrie, Pat. *The Architect's Portable Handbook*. New York: McGraw-Hill, 1995.

Hall, Edward T. *The Hidden Dimension*. New York: Doubleday, 1966.

Heyer, Paul. *Architects on Architecture: New Directions in America*. New York: Random House, 1993.

Hirsch, Dr. Allan R. *Scentsational Weight Loss*. New York: Simon and Schuster, 1998.

Kinetics Noise Control Design Manual. Dublin, OH: Kinetics Noise.

Leibrock, Cynthia, and Behar, Susan. *Beautiful Barrier-Free: A Visual Guide to Accessibility*. Bethesda, MD: Van Nostrand Reinhold, 1993.

Liberman, Jacob. *Light: The Medicine of the Future*. Rochester, VT: Inner Traditions, 1992.

McLuhan, Marshall. *Understanding Media: The Extensions of Man*. Cambridge, MA: MIT Press, 1994.

Mojay, Gabriel. *Aromatherapy for Healing the Spirit*. Rochester, VT: Healing Arts Press, 2000.

Niehoff, Debra. *The Biology of Violence: How Understanding the Brain, Behavior, and Environment Can Break the Vicious Cycle of Aggression*. New York: Free Press, 1999.

Overton, Donald. Philadelphia: Temple University.

Pert, Candace B., PhD, and Chopra, Deepak. *Molecules of Emotion: Why You Feel the Way You Feel*. New York: Scribner, 1997.

State of Illinois Capital Development Board. *Illinois Accessibility Code*. April, 1997.

Susanka, Sarah, and Obolensky, Kira. *The Not So Big House: A Blueprint for the Way We Really Live*. Newtown, CT: Taunton Press, 1998.

Wright, Frank Lloyd, and Hitchcock, Henry Russell. *In the Nature of Materials: The Buildings of Frank Lloyd Wright 1887–1941*. New York: Da Capo Press, 1942.

Wydra, Nancilee. *Feng Shui: The Book of Cures*. Lincolnwood, IL: Contemporary Books, 1996.

Wydra, Nancilee. *Feng Shui and How to Look Before You Love: Feng Shui Techniques for Revealing Anyone's True Nature*. Lincolnwood, IL: Contemporary Books, 1998.

Wydra, Nancilee. *Feng Shui for Children's Spaces*. Lincolnwood, IL: Contemporary Books, 2001.

Wydra, Nancilee. *Feng Shui Goes to the Office*. Lincolnwood, IL: Contemporary Books, 2000.

Wydra, Nancilee. *Feng Shui in the Garden*. Lincolnwood, IL: Contemporary Books, 1997.

Wydra, Nancilee. *101 Ways Feng Shui Can Change Your Life*. Chicago: Contemporary Books, 2002.

Organizations

Clear Your Space . . . Clear Your Mind
Linda Parks
922 Elmwood Avenue
Evanston, IL 60202
Phone: (847) 328-4556 or (847) 293-2992
Fax: (847) 425-1780
E-mail: ljparks@attglobal.net
Declutter expert

Feng Shui Institute of America (FSIA)
Nancilee Wydra
P.O. Box 488
Wabasso, FL 32970
Phone: (888) 488-FSIA (3742)
Fax: (561) 589-1611
E-mail: windwater8@aol.com
Websites: www.windwater.com (for information about feng shui professional educa-
tion and a list of consultants worldwide); www.efengshuiusa.com (for *free* feng shui
information)
Feng shui professional training

Feng Shui Institute International (FSII)
7547 Bruns Court
Canal Winchester, OH 43110
Phone: (614) 837-8370
Fax: (614) 834-9760
E-mail: fengshuimasters1@aol.com
Website: fengshuiinstituteinternational.com
Membership organization for feng shui professionals trained by FSIA

Full Circle Architects, LLC
Lenore Weiss Baigelman
1510 Old Deerfield Road, Suite 201
Highland Park, IL 60035
Phone: (847) 831-0884
Fax: (847) 831-1055
E-mail: lenorewb@aol.com or lenore@fullcirclearchitects.com
Website: www.fullcirclearchitects.com
Architects and interior designers approaching design from every angle, especially the
human angle

International Institute for Bau-Biologie & Ecology
Helmut Ziehe
1401 A Cleveland Street
Clearwater, FL 33755
Phone: (727) 461-4371
Fax: (727) 441-4373
E-mail: baubiologie@earthlink.net
Website: www.bau-biologieusa.com
Information on creating healthy conditions in a home

Index